Telegnosis

"Ancient Indian Predictive Science"

Himanshuray Raval
"Haqeer"

KORYFI GROUP
of Media & Publications

Telegnosis

"Ancient Indian Predictive Science"

Author: Himanshuray Raval "Haqeer"

ISBN: 978-81-962031-5-3

Price: Rs. 500/-

First Edition: July 2023
Second Edition: May 2024

Publisher & Printer:

Koryfi Group of Media and Publications
Address: B-515, 5th Floor, Shalin Square, Nr. Lalgebi Circle,
S. P. Ring Road, Hathijan, Ahmedabad, Gujarat, India - 382445
Phone: +91-635 635 60 70 | **Email:** editor@koryfigroup.org
Website: www.koryfigroup.org

Cover Designer:
Dr. Brahmaghosh Raval

Foreword

"The best way to predict the future is to study the past or prognosticate" Robert Kiyosaki.

There are many great predictors like Nostradamus, but prediction is not an easy business for a layman. It can be done by knowledgeable person using his wisdom, insight and in-depth knowledge.

Telegnosis, the word itself is not much known but it implies mastery over so many areas of knowledge, joined together and incorporated with intuition, they provide you miraculous results. It is for the first time that Mr. Himanshuray Raval has ventured to dive deep into this subject and has thrown light various techniques to diagnose a person using what we call intuition, knowledge of Astrology, Ayurved, Physiognomy and what not, to enable the master to predict about the person with accuracy.

In India, majority of the people believe in Astrology which is a science, based on the movement of constellations, but this different kind of science and technique involves experimentation. Telegnosis is a unique technique which is still in a growing state.

Recently, the prediction of Baba Dhirendra Shastri of Bageshwar Dham and his method of telling history and future of a person without knowing or seeing him, has opened Pandora's box. We don't know about his 'modus operandi' but here is a science – Telegnosis, which does not claim but proves that the methods adopted by the experiments of it would definitely be fruitful and beneficial to human kind. Like all miraculous sciences, Telegnosis also is a subject of faith and belief which can be performed successfully by a person with pure conscience and intuition. The positive results can help the department of Health, Police, Judiciary, Agriculture, and businessmen.

Who would not like to know about what is going to happen in his life tomorrow ? This curiosity to know about future makes man spend thousands of rupees to fortune-tellers and astrologers.

Telegnosis is a science based on meticulous calculations, conjecture, effective communication, and the art of decoding the person's situation and signals. This science has its support in Atharva Sootra and Brihat Samhita. As the author has done concrete research on this topic and has brought out many relevant truths, hopefully the book will definitely help those who are curious to know more about the occult sciences. Here, Telegnosis tries to prove its claims with 'Pratyaksh Pramaan' and hence, this new science requires more and more experimental research, based on scientific methods.

This book has opened new vista to ponder over seriously with a new perspective on various nuances of Indian Knowledge System. Mr. Himanshuray Raval has made a new beginning to arouse curiosity of many intellectuals and this book is going to provide an impetus and would also work as a catalyst to bring out more and more subtle truths about the scientific methods of knowing the future or predicting the future of someone on the basis of Telegnosis.

Although the knowledge of future may be fruitful as well as it may prove to be perilous. In Sanskrit, it is said that अथवा भावितव्यानाम् द्वाराणि भवंति सर्वत्र। (Abhigyan Shakuntalam).

Still predictions are significant as the weather predictions about the economic trends and possibility of fluctuations in GDP, all these matter even to Nation's future. An individual can take decisions about his or her life and can prepare a proper road-map if he or she gets some help and guidance by the wise predictors.

I wish the book gets worthy readers and they practice and experiment the methods and make their experiences richer and others' life better with Telegnosis techniques then only the purpose of the author will be served. Such books create ripples amongst the common stream flowing without any scruples. New patterns based on scientific attitudes always bring positive changes in the minds of the people and ultimately the society feels the positive vibes.

Wish all success to the author and the readers.

शुभास्ते सन्तु पंथानः

Dr. Shruti Kikani Anerao
11th April 2023

(Professor at Gujarat Technological University, Ahmedabad, and Professor in Charge of the Project 'Dharohar' to promote Indian Knowledge Systems)

Preface

If we ask a fish in the Pacific Ocean whether it is connected with fishes in the Indian Ocean, it will say no, but we know that the Oceans are one; and that the waters do connect all these fishes, so is the case of every living being, including fishes and birds and vegetation: we are all connected due to the Aakash or Ether. For this reason, the trees shed and wear leaves in anticipation of forthcoming season. Similarly, the shoals of fishes, the huge flocks of birds, groups of deer, sheep, cows, dogs etc., are often seen moving together for a purpose, and that too in a very disciplined way, matching only with an Army parade! In the famous Brihat Samhitaa, it is said that the king should carefully appoint Chief Astrologer, supported by four good astrologer-staff who are well-versed in every such behaviour, forming LakshaN. Albironi has translated some part of this huge volume of 100 chapters and about 4000 metres like Anushtup and Shaardool-aveekridit. I remember to have read in some old book that people should prefer to stay in that kingdom where there are good astrologers. Despite this, the world remains a great confusion for a scientific man.

This indicates that there exist languages in the nature that we, humans, often fail to understand. Further, some common language of communication is also likely to be existing which saves life before actual tsunami or earthquake etc. Indian Sages have worked on all these. The common factor, connecting all of us, is named as Atharvaa Sootra. Telegnosis tries to understand this Atharvaa Sootra and tries to foretell something useful with regard to a genuine question in human mind. Brihat Samhitaa, the famous compilation in India, says that an astrologer must predict in light of Hora, Horoscope, Muhoort, LakshaN (omens seen in the burning quarters of Sun), Lunar date, Day etc.

Generally, questions are put directly to astrologer, lawyer or doctor, but in this big world, it is not possible to consult personally. Famous doctors abroad can also be approached, today. Telegnosis is always with regard to specific question, put directly to astrologer or through his representative. The experiment shows that this works wonders even when this chain is longer: A querist sends his representative to a doctor (or a lawyer) and the question is finally put by him to the astrologer. This still brings useful answers.

Telegnosis is a technique to find the best possible option available to an individual with regard to a real situation. Based on this method, any question can be effectively answered without having working knowledge of the field to which the question is related. Telegnosis is a mix of so many methods, successfully used by me to provide a timely reply, after crosschecking the same, and with minimum mistakes. We have to accept that science of Fingerprints has helped the judiciary substantially and now Graphology is one such fast coming up branch which has potential to predict many things about writer even in his absence; and that such methods should also form part of Telegnosis. Since I have observed this to be a very cost-effective method, I wish to share it with all.

We may have to note that though Sages have compiled a huge literature on foretelling by using different methods, for most, it is like words of a teacher; and unless we work on it, the meaning will not dawn on us. Simply by reading a book on anatomy a hundred times, one cannot become a medical surgeon. To learn Statistics, one must learn mathematics first, and the reverse is not possible. We cannot expect any further simplification of the subjects to our satisfaction!

I see it like this that Nature addresses all of us, including birds, animals and even trees, in some common language like a mother talks to her child. In addition to that common language, Chhaayaa, Svar, LakshaN, Palmistry, Jyotish (Horoscopy and Horary), Numerology, are the additional languages that each child may pick up from his playmates. It is a fact that these branches of knowledge are original contributions made by scholars for the benefit of all. The present forms of these sciences are result of a correction process going on for centuries; and will still continue. Telegnosis is all about taking advantages of such time-tested results which are available as oral traditions, or in the form of books.

I am only trying to show usefulness and cost effectiveness of Telegnosis in different walks of life where many individuals live below the Poverty Line – for whom, the costs are unaffordable and Telegnosis can reduce financial burden, and the tensions caused by that burden.

When I talk about Telegnosis, an impression is created that it is the result of years of meditation. The doctors in the West, in the initial stage, thought that I was talking about some mystic powers; so was the response when it was opened up for a few participants at Vankaner (near Rajkot) and in Ahmadabad some years ago! All thought that no one will be able to understand the Telegnosis, leave aside the idea of experimenting it successfully on that very day! But it is Science. Science did work, and many could witness the extent of accuracy from their own eyes! In view of this, I am sure that, Telegnosis, if practiced for an appropriate time, say a decade or so, will certainly help. I recommend it's use in health, crime, judiciary, agriculture, insurance, business transactions, marriage etc., as well as in our routine daily life.

It is interesting to note that since many branches of astrology join to form Telegnosis, a study of this method will bring us face to face with many new subjects like Chhaayaa shaastra, Svar shaastra. Though each subject is a life time career, I feel that the reader will enjoy even these introductory presentations.

As we said earlier, Jyotish is like a small lamp in hand of a querist, travelling in a proverbial pitch-dark night; and that a lamp cannot be expected to show everything that a person could see in presence of Sun. Telegnosis increases the area, illuminated by that lamp; but it is a lamp anyway. Prudent astrologers know that planets only indicate and never cause events. But the general scenario is quite different, and the Planets are being worshipped for causing an event by performing Shaanti-poojaa etc! Astrologers are to be blamed for this. Such things bring a bad name to the Science. Time has come to simplify this subject and bring it within the reach of common man's logic. It is not difficult at all. But I agree there still will remain unsolved riddles: Suppose a child asks that why the water of oceans does not settle down due to gravitational forces like it does in a pot or a pond or a tank, though all are equally exposed to the same wind! Studies show that the percentage of twin delivery is much higher in Negro Race! We do not have answers to many such things yet.

I am thankful to Dr. Sudhir Shah, the eminent Neurologist and a Padma Awardee medical scholar, to constantly keep me inspired, and for taking one session on Palmistry as related with medical diagnosis. I am thankful to Dr. Saurabh Chokshi, MD, firstly for his participation in the formal study on Telegnosis (2022), and secondly for addressing the participants through his video-recording of summary of the Study findings. I am also thankful to Dr. Melinda Toney, Dr. Arati Shah, both from US, who encouraged me to scale up the study of Telegnosis; I thank Shri Mahendrabhai Raval, my guru; and also Shri Pinakin Raval, Shri Mukesh Parekh, Smt. Jaldhara Pandya and Dr. Sunil Pandey, whose discussions kept me well-directed; I also thank Ms. Shikha Sharma for her support in compiling this book in proper order; and I also thank Prof. Dr. Shruti Anerao, the Officer in charge of Dharohar Project at Gujarat Technological University, Ahmedabad, the biggest University in Gujarat today, for providing a platform (30 January to 27 March 2023) to this entirely new subject. I am highly indebted to authors of ancient Indian sciences, and all my words will fall short of expressions for the works of Sages like Varah Mihir, Paraashar, Charak, Sushrut, Vaagbhat, Harihar (Prashn Marg, commentary given by Late Shri B V Raman), translators of Prashn Gyaan, Bhuvan Deepika, Prashn Saar, Hathayogapradeepika and Yog Shatak; and the various publications on PuraaN like VishNu PuraaN.

It is of great importance that All India Council for Technical Education, and Gujarat Technological University, have started giving more and more importance to the Indian Knowledge Systems in every possible way! This will take us to newer heights of the civilisation.

I dedicate this book to Brishti, my grand daughter, my knowledge-hungry child, who allowed me to write this book because it was 'my homework'.

Himanshuray Raval
B 1001, Satyamev Vista, Near S. G. Highway, Gota, Ahmedabad 382481
(Mobile number 9429202015)
himanshurayraval@gmail.com

27 March 2023
6th Chaitri Navaratri

Preface to
Second Edition

Dear Readers,

I am thankful for the heartening response to the first edition of Telegnosis. It is heartening that Gujarati translation of this book is already published by Gujarat Technological University, Ahmedabad, and they have distributed about 500 copies as text-book under National Education Policy, 2024. All have agreed that the presentation of such complex concepts has been found useful in the easy language - which is otherwise to be obtained from the scattered libraries, often difficult to reach.

I am thankful to Shri Sameer Raval, and Parul devi for pointing out some 5 – 6 errors, inadvertently left in the first edition. In fact, proof reading of such technical material has typical limita-tion; good that my attention was drawn by these well-wishers. I hope, this version will serve the purpose of a ready reckoner for future researchers and scholars for propagating better de-cision-making with the help of Ayurved and Indian Astrology.

Himanshuray H Raval   05 May, 2024
B 1001, Satyamev Vista
Off S G Highway, Near Gota Underpass
Gota, Ahmedabad 382481

Index

Introduction

The word 'Telegnosis' does appear in Google and it is used to indicate an information, or an information - obtained in advance, from a distance, to be used for corrective measures, if any. What we are going to see is very close to this concept. For us, Telegnosis means obtaining information from a distance in reply to a genuine question put before us politely with a view to getting guidance.

Diagnosis = Person/ Patient >> Doctor/ Lawyer.
Telegnosis = Person/ Patient >> Agent >> Doctor/ Lawyer
>> Astrologer.

It is said that all living animals emit energy called Alpha, Beta, Gama rays, and it is said that it is more so in cases of humans who are in meditative stage. In view of this, it is possible that these rays must be getting absorbed or received by someone or somewhere. It, therefore, is possible that the receiver could understand and act upon the communication! Since we are all connected by Ether, this should be logically possible. Telegnosis is an effort to decode the subtle signals and communications with regard to a question.

Generally, our mind is full of problems at all points of time; and issues are either related to health or some type of crime or misbehaviour with us. We often see in cases of many friends that the same disease or misunderstanding or criminal case goes on even for decades! We keep spending heavily in solving problems in many ways mainly because we do not know the best alternative! Either the best medicine is not available, or the best doctor is yet to meet, or the best lawyer is not in picture. The bill paid on medicines and lawyers is in the range of five to seven digits! The question is how many middle class families can really afford such expenditure and time-lag? It is a huge cost. Medicine and Pharma are the biggest business in the world with a volume of over $ 800 billion US per year (2015) growing @14% and involving about 25 billion patients. Being the most powerful business, they are able to change definitions of diseases and the various benchmarks of health to their advantage. This business volume would have doubled by now! We must expect doctors to be so equipped that the need for pathological test should not be more than 5% of total expenditure on treatment at national level! All know that despite advancements in medical miracles, the expenditure (Income of Pharmaceutical companies) is growing at almost 15%. What kind of advancement is this: The life should have become easier! The cure should have become cheaper! Telegnosis can readily provide information about the best possible medicine, doctor etc., at any stage! Let it be tried as a second opinion, if not as mentioned in books of Ayurved. Telegnosis can certainly help without any cost and without any time lag! What is wrong in testing the invaluable treasure already scattered in our old books! We should not reject Telegnosis simply because it is available originally in Sanskrit, let us remember that Sanskrit, like English today, was the language of top brains of the world when these books were authored. Let me add that, Telegnosis can address issues outside medical and criminal areas also, and the benefit in terms of feel-good factor will be immeasurable. At this stage, **I propose to place Telegnosis as a tool to take**

'second opinion' in the field of health and crime.

It needs to be noted that though Telegnosis is rooted in Ayurved and also in some PuraaN, written in Sanskrit, and is also a part of Course Curriculum for Graduate degree in Ayurved, it is painful to see that the doctors are not able to establish its importance before the modern medicine world. If applied, it will add to reputation of Ayurved.

I am yet to see any textbook on Allopathy or Homeopathy which is written in perfect poetry! It is because these expert founders were just doctors! The writers of Ayurved were all multifaceted. Integrated approach to learning has been a feature of Indian Knowledge System and that Sages were not only masters of technical sciences like Medicine, Astronomy, Mathematics, but were equally well versed in poetic presentations of these subjects. Let us see if some medical professor could write English Medicine or Surgery in Ballad or Sonnet or Pentameter as per grammar of English Poetry! This lacuna seems to have led to a kind of envy inasmuch as the West has ignored even the contents of Ayurved simply because it is presented in poetic form! For them, Science and Literature are two different things, but in India, all ancient scholars have been experts in every branch of knowledge, and that without such versatility, they were not classified as scholars. Let it not happen anymore, common people on the earth need knowledge. We may not like a language, but we must not miss the knowledge available there.

We all should agree that the West has produced good mechanical and robotic support; and we should accept the advancement. The time has come that they also start respecting the bare-handed experts in India who wrote books like

Soorya Samhitaa, Ayurved, Atharv Ved; who knew everything about Eclipse etc., much before days of RaamaayaN and Mahaabhaarat, long before Jesus, and certainly much before Galileo, and Newton and such other respectable names.

Today, thanks to the printing and computer technology, we have all texts in hands without much costs; hence, now calculating the position of Planets and the degree of Ascendant with regard to a birth chart or Horary chart, and the various Dashaa, Antaradashaa etc. incidental to the same, is not a problem at all. Computer takes care of all these things that were considered to be very time-taking and cumbersome during those days. Now, what is important is to make near accurate predictions. This has always required some inner character of the astrologer. The basic practice of sharpening the mind and concentration is the missing link. Without this, there is no difference between Astrology and Arithmetical calculations. We can develop the acumen by training our mind in some daily practice as suggested separately.

Further, Telegnosis happens to be in conformity with India's sole National Agriculture Policy, published in the year 2000 (Nov), which says that we need to explore and use the local knowledge to predict so many things. Many experts have conducted many experiments to compare rains in Gujarat, based on Machines and also on Texts written in books on Parjanya Vidya, authored by Sages like Varah Mihir. He has found that accuracy is much higher when we take into consideration the wisdom of Varah Mihir. I, therefore, feel that we need to seriously study Telegnosis and apply the principles in our day to day life to live a healthy and cost-effective life.

Telegnosis and Crime

From the time immemorial, human societies have been having two important sectors under government: Medicines, and Crime and Justice. Order of the world has changed with mass industrialization, shifting the focus from man to mass production, the methods of treating the ill, and dealing with criminals have also changed. These sectors have become like industries. It is useful to recall that in modern India, we have introduced local governance by adopting Panchayat Raaj, seen with reference to revenue and implementation of Law.

India has always believed that people should be healthy and should feel safe that wrong-doers will get punished quickly. We had systems of obeying the Rulings of the elders in family, some issues were resolved by the Mukhi or the wisest person in the village, and business issues were resolved by leaders of each community. Thus, only a few issues went up to the Administrators and Kings! After implementing the English systems, the lower levels of problem resolving machinery are destroyed by calling it not proper! They want us to forget that India had practically no crimes and frauds due to efficiency of those lower levels of judiciary systems. If today's system is to be branded better, then why there are about 8 crore cases pending in different courts! Unfortunately, no figures are available with regards to fees charged by lawyers per case, the per case expenditure and hearings etc. How do we justify that this system is working well! Many people die in jails awaiting verdict, many keep fighting cases for the entire life or even for three – four decades! Can we call it a better system? Is not something basically wrong here?

The way cases are fought in Courts today, indicates that at least 50% are certainly siding with the wrong, that too on a very costly platform. Naturally, both sides cannot be innocent. This means that system has made it legal for criminals to fight for what they call Justice. Further, the judges are generally not allowed to investigate on their own, and they stay away from investigation. Everything is left to the professional lawyers, one is allowed to prove the crime, and more importantly the other is certainly allowed to present the case to cover the crime! Further, the system allows witnesses to change their statements and turn hostile: What can be more shocking than this permissible crime! Is it what we call a better judicial system! Further, when the higher court rejects the judgement given by a lower court, why that judge is not removed! He should be thrown out immediately for he has brought defame to the system. Who will respect such an immature judiciary tomorrow? On the other hand, many a time, Police are forced to arrest anyone related to a particular crime, they are at liberty to put them behind the bar merely based on a doubt. Maybe they will arrest entire family of the person who is likely to have committed crime! Naturally, over a period of time, most of them will be released or given bail by the Courts. They, when come out, come out with a stamp of a criminal on their personality. Naturally, this has added many frustrated persons in India today, thanks to the modern judicial system!

In Japan, the conviction rate is as high as 99%, while the rest of the world is near 55 to 60% conviction rate! In this background should not we study Japanese systems and improvise ours?

In India, Nyaay (Justice – with specific regard to application of Law) is defined as the fact that is in the overall interests of the society. For example, if a cow is coming running in my compound to hide, and if I misguide the butcher to a wrong direction; whether I have committed a crime! Yes, I did lie to butcher, but Indian System would not consider me as a criminal. Today's Indian courts of Law admit the evidences presented by the smart lawyers and evaluate the same to give a judgement in light of Laws enacted by Govt. of India. Due to competitive lifestyle, crimes are on an increase. The police are expected to file charge-sheets within 90 days of FIR, and book the criminals as soon as possible: In fact, there are chances that they 'frame' people, while they are trying to 'charge' the criminals! The witnesses, turning hostile, are not put behind the bar. In some countries, the FIR is supported by video of witnesses so there are less chances of witness's turning hostile so easily. It is possible that the courts are under pressure to 'save' someone depending on the political elections. It is also a fact that judges are not removed if the higher court rejects or overrules their verdict.

Appointment of Judges is made based on academic tests. What prudence could be expected of persons appointed as a judge at age 25 approx.! Only information on Law is not sufficient for an appropriate judgement, here, the entire life of the accused people is at their mercy. These judges naturally know nothing outside the campus of their Law college. They apply that information to write Judgements! It is like a singer singing all songs in just one tune that he knows!

I recall my experience about the impracticable approach that young judges adopt. My relative was a young Judge and he was transferred to another place. When staff had carefully rearranged all belongings and we all sat for dinner in that bungalow, suddenly we heard a lot of women screaming at top of their voices just close to the rear compound wall! My relative summoned the Police Inspector and gave him the orders to stop torture. It was learnt that tribal labourers were camping there in the vacant land behind the place, who returned drunk as a routine. Anyway, the officer agreed to stop torture and left with a thud of salute.

For about three four days, there was no screaming, rather there was such a silence that no one seemed to be staying there. My relative said that such was the power of Justice, and this and that and a hundred more things in favour of Administration. I was very young and was really impressed by the Administrative powers. Next afternoon, I saw about thirty ladies were asking permission of the Police constable standing at the gate to allow them to meet 'Madam'. I was worried like my aunty. Police constable told my aunty that they were the ladies who stayed behind the wall and wanted to make a submission. On realizing that the issue was social, they were allowed to enter. They silently sat on the floor. I went inside and called by aunty. All illiterate and poor ladies greeted my aunty in a very respectful way. The real surprise came when my aunty asked them to tell the reason of this delegation! The elderly lady told that because of the order, their husbands had stopped beating them every evening, and that was the entire problem! My aunty congratulated them, and being a post graduate scholar, told them all about the ideal and peaceful married life, and the good impact of such a life on children and like that. The women listened to her carefully. A woman then said 'Madam, if your husband did not like you that does not mean that my husband does not love me!' This was quite out of the box for us, me and my aunty. We were clearly confused. The other lady, therefor, clarified that 'drinking liquor and wife beating was a normal pre dinner tradition in their families for generations', rather it was part of their lifestyle insomuch as if the husband did not beat his wife, something was certain to have gone wrong'. For them, such beating was clearly a proof of intimacy! And by stopping that practice, my relative had destroyed the family life of those fifty families, inadvertently though! What is good and just for one, cannot be so for the other. Judges must have experience of life, passing an examination is not sufficient. Hence in India, Justice was defined as the standpoint which helps the majority in the society. By freeing the criminals simply because there is no clear evidence is encouraging the criminals to commit crimes in such a way that the Law cannot reach them! The crime has almost become an industry because of this modernity, and jails have become training centres for the future criminals who learn about the loopholes in the system.

Raag Paad Ne Paarakhu, Naadi Ne VaLi Nyaay
Taravu, Taskaravu, Taatarvu, Aathee Aap Kalaay

Among other things, this Gujarati couplet presents the basic feature of a good doctor and a good judge. It says that Naadi (Pulse of a living person that is the reference to medical expertise) and Nyaay (System to deliver justice) are among the eight in-born talents. No doubt, training and exposure in these fields enhance the acumen, but still these sectors require gifted people. Telegnosis equips them better by teaching them the methods to frame sub questions in the Courts as per procedure. Telegnosis quickly takes onc to the appropriate questions that will instantly unearth the truth.

Let us have a bird's eye view of history of Astrology. It is generally said that it was systematically presented in Egypt around 500 BC, that started taking systematic form around

325 BC – the time of Alexander the Great. It is called Hellenistic Astrology. It refers to drawing of a Natal chart, interpret the position of stars in those 12 Houses, and predict major aspects of future life of a particular person. They say that by that time about 7000 sets of calendrical omens were available in that category of literature. Some say that this compilation started around 1800 BC. Without any intention to compare this with Indian literature, I recall that our Samhitaa like Bhrigu, Varah Mihir and many others, have much older verses on Omens, called LakshaN! It is said that a few psychologists like Jung made efforts to bring in Astrological aspects and Kinesics in the definition of diagnosis but experiments by some high-level committees, comprising doctors and astrologers, could not prove that astrology was any help. However, nothing could be disproved.

It is with this background, that we make a beginning to understand each of the major styles of answering genuine questions. Horoscopy, and to a large extent, Horary astrology are the two mathematical methods, while the others like LakshaN, Svar, Chhaayaa, Numerology, Lamp, are nonmathematical methods. Both need to be studied and applied to increase accuracy.

Notes

____

____

____

____

____

India & Astronomy

Time is a continual phenomenon, and no one can perfectly understand it. Over a period, man has come out with different methods of measuring Time in some units that do not differ much. It is 'seen' as a flowing river which produces sound like 'Kal-Kal'. From this expression, the words like Kaal, Calculation and Calculus seem to have been derived! Though it is a continued thing, man has tried to break it into units, and has been making sincere effort to identify the best time to do certain things, for example humans take lunch and dinner at almost same part of the day in all countries and in all civilizations and avoid travelling in night. In a book called 'Itihaasachakra' Dr. Lohia writes that "The time, past, is present in future". We can see that while examining a Chart, an astrologer, while predicting something, does touch upon causes that brought that problem to the querist, maybe either as his deeds in past birth or his past karm in this existence.

Over a period, Man identified Dhruv or Pole star and evolved maps, and road maps to travel to some other places of world. First such expertise is found in RaamaayaN where we find that Sugreev is well versed in guiding soldiers about places across the Globe, in all four directions though he was seated in central India. Some authors have shown how ancient navigators could have made sea routes with use of ropes, called

Aksh (later adopted as Axis). The pictorial presentation of Sun God as having seven horses, a chariot on two wheels, each having six supports is an excellent proof of knowledge of Sun rays' having 7 colours, the two Ayan (Uttaraayan and DakshiNaayan) causing six seasons. The knowledge of Ayan is a vocal proof that they knew about the tilted axis of Earth. Agni puraaN says that Astrology is an exercise that suggests to us that what is good and what is not so good, if done at a given time! It is believed that the Vedic literature is the oldest in the history of human civilization, and astronomical knowledge was a part of it. Perhaps, Man used to initially thank Rain God, Sun God, Moon God, Fire God, Water God, Wind God whenever the seasons were changing. They used to perform Yajn like Ishtika, Darsh-PourN, Vaajapey, which clearly show their correct astronomical information. This might have added Indra, Rudra and many others as Gods. The litcrature is full of prayers for a blissful life for everyone in general. This resulted in concept of dividing the entire universe around Earth into 12 Raashi and 27 Nakshatra. It is beyond our imagination that how expertly and intelligently, Sages have assigned representation of almost everything to these Raashi and Nakshatra. Similar is the astrological assignment of friendship, colour, nature, metals, directions, jurisdiction, their inter se aspects, their being beneficial in certain celestial position etc. The word Chhaayaa is also used as unit of calculation of shadow of a rod, fixed perpendicular in the land to measure its shadow at different points of Sunlight and calculate the time, as given in the chapter on Astronomy. There it is related to unit of time. It is interesting to note that instead of 12 Raashi, entire Universe is divided into 27 constellations, again clubbed into 9 main groups viz., Janm, Sampatkar, Vipatkar, Kshemya, Pravar, Saadhak, Naidhan, Mitra and Paramamitra. Thus, calculation of time is considered more important. The time equal to 12 blinking of eye is equal to one Lav, 360 Lav make one Kalaa, 30 Kalaa are equal to one Truti; and 30 Truti make one Muhoort.

With reference to Vedic period, the word Muhoort presupposes knowledge of orbits of Earth and Sun both. Shatapath Brahman reads that the path of Sun is known as Pathya Svasti, as it forms four different angles with Saptarshi when taken at 90 degree every three months, making it 360-degree circle, denoted as 'Svastik'. In Yajurved, these degrees are named as Rashmi. This knowledge shows that in ancient India, we had complete understanding of all major celestial movements and their impact on Earth, and agriculture; and activities were accordingly conducted. For every God (giver), different types of Yajn were performed which were more of thanks giving ceremonies than anything else.

As believed generally, Man has been in search of the best time for commencing certain activity. All big kings, including Alexander the Great, used to request noted astrologer to be in the army camps. This is how the Electional Astrology might have come into existence. There is a method of finding Muhoort on any day in any season.

A rod of 12 Angul (one angul is the breadth of middle digit of middle finger of an average adult) is used in general. At the Sun-rise, the shadow is equal to 96 angul. As the Sun rises, till the shadow is 60 angul, it is called Roudra Muhoort; up to 12; it is called shvet; up to 7 is Maitra; up to 6 it is Saarbhat; when 5 angul, it saavitra; up to 4 is Vairaaj; up to 3 it is Vishvaavasu; when there is no shadow, it is called Abhijit Muhoort; then starts the afternoon. When the shadow is 3 angul, it is called RouhiN Muhoort; up to 4, it is called Bal, then comes the most famous Muhoort called Vijay Muhoort which is up to the time the shadow has become 5 angul; followed by Nairut till 6 angul; when shadow is 12 angul it is Vaarun; up to 60 angul it is Saumya Muhoort; and the last one is Bhag or Godhooli Muhoort. In general, Shvet, Maitra, Saavitra, Abhijit, Vijay and Bhag are considered good for making good beginning and for compromise etc. In Telegnosis, these Muhoort can form part of advice. Logically, in winter, a Muhoort will be smaller than the same in Summer. Since there is no shadow in the night, and because the ancient Indians hardly took up any major activities in the night, Muhoort were more relevant for the day time. For centuries, therefore, many astrologers have adopted that a Muhoort is a unit of 48 minutes, irrespective of the shadow which is the time taken by Sun to illuminate one thirtieth of the rotating Earth. The system of Hora seems to be equally old and more acceptable as compared to Muhoort. Both are used to find the most suitable time for a specific activity.

After that stage, they might have started thanking other Gods for some favour in small battles for areas of operation and property of sorts in conformity with changing social set up. It is felt that their calculations were more based on the 27 constellations called 'Gandharva'. The term astrology therefore, in fact, is to be seen in much larger way. It is thought that the era of astronomical interpretations of planetary positions and the period of electional astrology both might have evolved as a part for ascertaining better or appropriate time for social activities as well. They might have also taken in view the various indications available in environment in the forms of LakshaN, Chhaayaa, Shagun, Nimitt, Svar shaastra, Ayurved, and many other things that we are going to discuss under Telegnosis.

Champions of pure Vedic philosophy hold that till it is Astronomy, it does form Eye of Ved, and astrological interpretation is not important. For this reason, Svami Dayanand Sarasvati, has advised that we may not study astrology for foretelling events and for Life-reading as printed in Newspapers.

It is to be noted that in India, Jyotish is used as Astronomy (change in a Tithi, or Lunar date) as well as for geographical use (impact of an Eclipse in an area); and was generally used for better agricultural production. We also have time-unit called Truti, which is less than a second (in Jain Aagam, the truti was much smaller, maybe one second divided by six hundred) ; but such fine calculations were perhaps for some astronomical mathematics and are certainly not used in Horary astrology which is our subject, today. When it was used in Astrology, India calculated Time as follows for predictions :-

- One respiration is equal to 4 seconds
- Six respirations or 24 seconds were equal to 1 Pal
- 60 Pal were equal to 1 Ghati and
- 2.5 Ghati was equal to 1 Hora.

In VishNu PuraaN, the calculation of time is as follows:-
- 15 Nimesh (Blinking of Eye in a normal person) is equal to 1 KaaShtaa
- 30 KaaShtaa are equal to one Kalaa
- 30 Kalaa are equal to one Muhoort; and
- 30 Muhoort are equal to one Ahoraatra (day and night from Sun-rise to Sun-rise).

In one Gujarati commentary, the definition of one Nimesh,

as given by Yaajnavalkya is given differently from this, but ultimately it leads to undisputable measure of one Hora, which has become the biggest gift of India, given to world.

In Atharv Vedeey Jyotisham, a book published by reputed temple of Datiyaa (in MP), the following measurement of time is given which is close to the first one given above:-

- 12 Nimesh are equal to one Lav (Dvaadashaakshi Nimeshastu Lavo)
- 360 Lav are equal to one Kalaa
- 30 Kalaa are equal to one Truti; and
- 30 Truti are equal to one Muhoort.

From above we observe two main words, Muhoort and Hora. We have discussed Muhoort in enough detail for its use here. About Hora, let us quickly see facts about the word Hora. **The English word 'Hour', a unit of time today, is undoubtedly derived from this Sanskrit word Hora.** What more should we say that how old our mathematics is! One more interesting fact, a Universal practice of naming the week days is also derived from the pattern set by Indian Sages in such a way that every twenty fifth hora will be the first hora of the next day, if calculated in the order of Ravi, Shukra, Budh, Vidu, Mand, Guru and Bhaum (Sun, Venus, Mercury, Moon, Saturn, Jupiter and Mars, respectively). There is no other explanation of this order of weekdays anywhere in the world. Let me add that two systems are presented in Svar Shaastra viz., Weekdays and Tithi (Lunar dates). Though Tithi is a truth that is equally applicable to planet Earth, irrespective of the differing Weekday in East and West due to Greenwich Mean Time; the Weekday system seems to be more effective as indicated in the first chapter of Prashn Marg.

While one Hora (hour) is equal to 60 minutes, the Muhoort is equal to the time taken by Sun to illuminate thirtieth part of the Earth (at Equator) which is close to 48 minutes, in general. In one Rashi, there are two Hora. If the Rashi is an odd number, the first Hora is ruled by Sun and second by Moon. Moon will rule the first Hora and Sun will rule the second, if the zodiacal sign is an even number. In view of this the method of measuring a Muhoort by using shadow of a rod, fixed in an even ground, where length of shadow is measured in the light of Sun, is not generally followed.

The point is that Bhaarat had complete knowledge of Astronomy and therefore it is certain that it is the motherland of Jyotish, popularly known as Horoscopy. To take the most important proof, in India, the word Grah is used for a planet. This word itself indicates that it is a body which holds and deals with gravitational aspects. Then we see that the first reference to Solar Eclipse is available in Rugved, the oldest literature of the World. There exist 18 famous Samhitaas like Soorya, Atri, Brihat, Yavan, Chyavan, Manu etc. which illuminate our path. As we explore the other aspects of that era, we see that in Bhaarat, the Tantra Shaastra is perhaps equally old. The prayers are similar though in more colloquial tone. This indicates that the class that preferred Tantra walked along the Vedic population, but with some difference. The list of deities is longer in Tantra, though the process seems to be similar, if not same! In Tantra, we find Panchopaachar, Shodashopaaachar, Rajopachaar poojan of deities with panchaang purashcharaN done either Homaatmak or Japaatmak. In Tantra, the Anushthan are generally done for nine days (called Navaratri) every four months when the Saptarshi make 90 degrees angle with reference to the previous quarter and the Dhruv star called Polar star. Thus, we have ample evidence that Bharat was the leader in use of mathematics about astronomical positions and astrological predictions. I may add that we need to respect the Samhitaa written by Sages like Bhrigu, but our sole submission is that we need to use other branches of Astrology also, so that predictions become still more reliable. After all, Rishi Bhrigu was a person and wrote his findings for humans in a language that humans could read and understand, but what about the other species? Universe must have a language for them also! The post Vedic literature therefore needs to be revisited in detail to know as to how these animals behave and how they save their lives! Telegnosis respects that language also.

In India, we have a very old tradition that can be traced back even to RaamaayaN days, the oldest possible historical epic of Indian subcontinent. In that tradition, there are ample references that Bhaarat (India) we had various types of Poojan, to be celebrated or performed by people very frequently; for example, we have poojan in almost 70 percent households either on every Ekadashi, every Amaavasya, every Poornima; some people perform pooja on every Monday and some on differing days of week. One thing that was common in all such common poojan, leave aside the special Yajn etc., that the priests used to intone the objective of each such poojan with the name of the person performing such poojan, his parentage, his geographical location in Jambudweep, the specific lunar date, the month, the week day, the specific season (of the six seasons in Bhaarat), the year of Manu, the presiding deity; and a few more features. This indicates that Indian priests had a daily update on Astronomical positions which speaks volumes that how easily we knew the advanced science and mathematics. It may be useful to know that such daily details are hardly available to any class of any society anywhere other than in Bhaarat! This is so because we had a dedicated class who valued importance of astronomy and were aware of the difference of time between the lunar and solar orbits. They had provided for Purushottam Month also known as Adhik Maas which adjusted the time difference between the orbits. The practice of having 28,29,30 and 31 days in Gregorian Calendar is not only absurd but is also not in tune with actual movements of Sun and Moon. Bhaaratiya calendar is scientific, and all knowledgeable people across the globe must agree. This proves that the people who knew such details cannot be and were not as backward as being depicted in books of history, today. They even knew that when a star would become retrograde and for what period.

RaamaayaN and Mahaabhaarat have astrological references to enable us to date the events, given in those books, but we also have independent books like Bhrigu Samhitaa that teach us art of drawing inference based in position of planets at the time of birth of a person! Though this has been challenged by Sages like Svami Dayanand, as not being in conformity with the Astrology presented in Ved, but still there are many who use that successfully. Further, it has been said to have been compiled by a great Sage by name of Bhrigu! There are many such Samhitaa in Bhaarat that teach us similar interpretations of birth charts. Anyone can read and learn from these Samhitaa that are still alive due to Bhaaratiya tradition of learning everything by heart, and not through books. It is just impossible to destroy Indian Knowledge Systems because of this tradition.

One can see that Yajurved records complete Decimal system in its 852 Shlok (Adhyaay 17). It is for us to accept that Indian Knowledge System needs to be revisited with an open mind so that all species in the world in general and human society, are benefitted for a meaningful survival. It takes altogether a different mind even to think of how they must have arrived at these patterns of tens, and Six (some Jain shaastra), and apply the same in their performance! It is difficult to fathom the depth of their mental reach, and their understanding of the Universe! We are only mesmerized by thinking of Einstein and Schrodinger and a few more who used the decimal system, let us think of the originators of Decimal system and we will realize the world beyond words.

The purpose of this chapter is to establish that since such excellent was the knowledge of bare-handed Vedic Rishis, the knowledge of all methods of foretelling, as available in Ayurved and Indian books on Jyotish, is certainly worth exploring.

Notes

Vaani & Pramaan

Types of Sound or audio communication
It will be useful to glance at the origin of questions. We all have questions, but we hardly think about how exactly the same originate. No one really knows what a thought is, and what is its language, how a thought enters the mind of any living being; and from where does it come! In India, Sound, language etc., are all studied under VaaNi. It is classified into four audio or audible sound frequencies, viz., Paraa, Pashyanti, Madhyamaa and Vaikharee. Let us have a glance over each because the question, with reference to Telegnosis, emanates from either of these four.

Paraa: *Paraaprakaashikaa Maayaa chaitanyaabhaas vishishtayaa*
Paraa is the first evidence of non-vibrating and illuminated manifestation of the Life. Such could be the definition of Paraa. There are experts who are able to read mind of others to a very great extent. They say that at all points of time, a living being keeps communicating its presence in its own way. We, humans, express ourselves through voice and movement etc., each animal has a typical smell, trees also have aura (Sachetanaaha Vrukshaaha). Kirilian photography, invented by a Russian scientist, is done to read the electrified air around

any living body, which is released by the living animal; this has colours, and the subject needs to be compared with the colours of Chhaayaa as referred to in books of Ayurved and Astrology in India. This may be conceptually different from the thermal images used by Military and Police to locate movements of humans and animals from a distance. A day will soon come when they will be able to see similar images of trees. It is common knowledge that in Tibet, experts train eyes for a long period to identify colour of flickers of light flashed in pitch dark. Let us know that such flickers appear only as white to an untrained eye, and we are able to identify colours because our eyes get longer exposure to light. Thus, the above definition takes us to believe that thoughts 'illuminate' Life, and that they may also have some smell! One such expert was able to smell a snake far behind him while being seated in a huge compound of a bungalow in a centrally located place in Rajkot in a dark night! The owner initially denied but when the lady came, she confirmed that a snake stayed in that direction of bungalow! It is agreed that Paraa is of academic interests for a beginner, but it is necessary to know that sound, basically is a vibration, that can be sensed in the form of light or smell, after special training.

The other three are in the form of vibrations.

Pashyanti: *Saspandaavasthaaha Pashyantaadyaaha.*
It is called BinduroopiNi. In Tantra, it is also indicated by way of a dot (on a Yantra) which is supposed to be the origin of all visible forms and all audible sounds! A point or a small dot is to be presumed as having no length or breadth or height or weight because such has to be the initial state of

life! In Ayurved, it is said that a prudent woman can know that she has conceived based on a typical vibration inside her womb. Pashyanti is also the language of extreme emotions, it is nothing but concentrated energy like a boon or a curse! Let us stop for a moment and recall that when we are extremely happy or upset, the mind experiences a huge traffic of words in our mind. Every such word is important and cannot be ignored, and that Emotion is just incomplete without that word! It could be exemplified by the emotion of a mother for her sick infant; and with the emotions of an animal being slaughtered. This is the form of Pashyanti and for this reason, it is considered concentrated energy, apparently in audio form. This state of mind is reflected in Chhaayaa and a trained eye can see changes taking place in our aura or Chhaayaa. This is the reflection of vibrations in terms of some units of heat or electricity or light or thermal energy.

Madhyamaa: *Bahyaantar KaaraNaatmika.*

Here, the sound frequency is associated with some organs of a living being. In animals, we observe that thoughts and emotions first get translated into actions of body, followed by appropriate sound or language. We see that from here starts importance of Kinesics or LakshaN. It is also to be noted that here actions come ahead of sound. Let us recall what happens when we are happy. The entire internal system is reset to celebrate by different secretions from different organs; nothing of this development is visible to us as such. Then, we start making some gestures, maybe a clap, tapping a foot, smile, raising hands, almost a dancing pose and like that. Then comes the stage of sound either as exclamations or words in Mother tongue. This happens so fast that we hardly know what came first! Similar is the case of animals, they generally dance or run or rush, before barking or creating sound from their respiratory systems.

It is said that this is VaaNi generated by some organs between naval point and the heart of animals. This means that it has relation with respiratory organs that vibrate the vocal cords to make sounds, audible to ears. It could be an ear of any species. What can be easily heard by a dog or a cow, is likely to be beyond capability of a human ear! Thus, Madhyamaa is the sound, that could be called a language in some form, which could be termed as a communication, maybe for a purpose.

Vaikharee: *Vaikharee NaadroopiNi.*
This is the audible sound. It is dependent on physical structure and age and strength of a living being. Humans have developed languages which are nothing but an age old practice to understand emotions in a particular community or region, without changing the expressions in Pashyanti, Madhyamaa and Paraa, as said above. It is said that over 80% of Vaikharee is understood by the intonation of words. Thus, the words and grammar and prosody of language are ornamental parts of Literature, and not those of a Language that Nature has gifted us to express.

For this reason, for a common man, no language is very difficult, for a good listener, no language is difficult, and for a saint, language is no bar at all.

There is huge literature and background to this subject in

Sanskrit language, in the books of Tantra; and an impressive account has been given by Hon'ble John Woodroffe in his English book, named Garland of Letters and also in Serpentine Power. There we find science of Mantra for specific purpose. Mantra is the single or complex sound, created mentally or vocally to create desired changes mostly in external environment. Today, we know that by creating frequencies, not audible to human ear, even big buildings can be destroyed, and discomfort can be created in human mind, and even heart attacks can be caused by matching someone's heart rate with a machine tuned with him! This gives an idea of how important the works of Sages could have been without use of machine before thousands of years. This also explains how Brahmastra or Agnyaastra or Krutyaa might have been fired during RaamaayaN and Mahaabhaarat Wars! Those Mantras were created or were 'seen' by Sages! Bhagavaan Parashuraam says that the best war is the one which is fought with Mantra, he is clearly indicating at use of Sound.

In Tantra, each sound is said to be 'ruling' a specific organ in human body, and that a process called Nyaas is prescribed for extending abilities of organs. Telegnosis does recognize strength of answers based on touch analysis as I shall try to discuss it in the relevant chapters. Here, it is sufficient to note that sounds have a capacity to prompt action and inspire a touch to certain organ. The literature on Sound or Mantra is poetically believed to have come to us as 'Aagam' and 'Nigam': 'Aagam' is gifted by Sun (God of Vibrations - light and sound), and from there has come the knowledge in various languages called 'Nigam'. Thus, Sun is the only source of Knowledge. In other words, it is said that supreme knowledge was first preached by Sun, and then it got disseminated for its use on Prithivi, the Mother Earth. There is another interpretation that Aagam is the knowledge which is subsequent to Ved, written mostly as dialogue between Bhagavaan Shankar and Mother Paarvati. Old Jain and Bauddh literature and most of the books of Tantra are also called Aagam. Aagam are generally considered as Aapt PramaaN. We need to remember that such fine aspects of Sound are also presented in very poetic expressions in the ancient Indian Knowledge System.

Under Telegnosis, we will see how Sages have used Sanskrit Alphabet for answering the questions. The Vowels and Consonants have been carefully classified and an explanation has been given as to which group of consonants indicates what! Likewise, a technique of predicting has been devised based on the first three short or long syllables, called GaN. The foregoing gives to us a deeper understanding of process of question from its origin till it is delivered to someone. As said elsewhere, it is not always possible to personally contact and consult prominent Astrologers, Doctors, Surgeons, Lawyers etc, due to various reasons like lack of time and money, long distance, but today modern apparatus like audio and video phones have largely won over these limitations. Maybe, with tomorrow's advancements, Teleportation will make it possible almost face to face meetings! Under Telegnosis, these modern techniques have been successfully used by this writer. The main reason for success is that a question, it's delivery, it's presentation etc., are far more important than the physical presence of the querist: Though personal meetings are the best.

PramaaN, types of evidence in Indian Knowledge System

Indian Knowledge Systems (IKS) always go by PramaaN. PramaaN generally refers to different types of evidence which form the basis for a science or philosophy or argument, as presented in ancient Indian books. Every Indian viewpoint tells the reader that on what kind of evidences, that particular thinking is presented. All societies generally adopt this system for day to day decision making with regard to agriculture, business, transportation, travel, crime detection etc. Sages, while propagating any theory, invariably state that based on what they have found that ideology to be true.

In India, all philosophies, including Ayurved, are presented strictly on the basis of Evidence (called PramaaN). The first Category is Pratyaksh PramaaN, Direct evidence or the first-hand experience refers to nothing but what is seen by one's own experienced eye etc. If a poet sees a cloud, it will be a poetry; if a farmer sees it, he may think of agriculture. A swelling, seen on hand by a doctor is different from the one seen by a mother! Thus, same evidence will reveal differing meaning and usefulness to different class of people. Astrologer is supposed to understand this fact with reference to questions put before him. We will try to understand this concept with specific reference to Ayurved because in astrology, most of the questions belong to health.

Ayurved is defined as a science that studies Life in every form. Ayurved is presumed to be an offshoot of Rugved. It has reference to the two brothers Ashvini Kumars. There is one old Samhitaa (edited collection of beneficial knowledge) called Aatrey Samhitaa, which means that either one or more persons belonging to holy linage of Sage Atri wrote and compiled it in about 25000 verses. This was presented by Charak in about 12000 verses. The Vaagbhat Samhitaa is one of the three great books on Ayurved, divided in eight main chapters (Kaay, Baal, Grah, Urdhvaang, Shaalya, Danshtra (Vish/Agad), Jaraa (Rejuvenation); and VaajikaraN; and seems to have been influenced by Aatrey Samhitaa. This is to show that how systematically the source of knowledge is being respected and preserved in India. It is seen that Ayurved is more of an inferential evidence, compiled based on inspiration and practice.

There are three main types of evidences Pratyaksh, Anumaan and Aapt. Summary as relevant to Telegnosis is given below:-

Pratyaksh PramaaN: This is nothing but direct evidence or something like being an Eyewitness. In other words, whatever that has been personally perceived through the five sensory organs which are normal and functional. The five sensory organs refer to touch on skin, taste in mouth, sound in ears, scene before the eyes and smell through nose. Let me quickly put Upamaan PramaaN in this category for the purpose of learning Telegnosis. In a disease, we see Masoorika, small pimple-like spread on skin that resembles the pulse called Masoor; hence the disease is called Masoorika. Here, the matter is explained based on what has already been seen by earlier scholars; and it is as good as one's personal observation. Today, if the Masoor like grains are shown to a doctor on a video call, or even narrated on an audio call, it can be classified as Pratyaksh PramaaN. The individual treating techniques of medicine of surgery copied or learnt from the senior is also Upamaan PramaaN.

Due to advancements in science, the area of Pratyaksh Pra-maaN is on an increase. Today, we have EEG, ECG, Sonography, DNA exercise, Radiology, Satellite Images of movements of Ocean currents and Wind velocity, some elaborate pathological reports, video films and CCTV footage of criminals and crime scenes; the fingerprint records etc., admitted even in the Courts of Law! But still almost in all spheres of life, we use inferential knowledge called Anumaan PramaaN. I do not know whether a Narco test is to be categorized as Pratyaksh or Anumaan, but it is a good tool to help decision making. To make it succinct, we can club the screen-based images in this category in medical context like X ray plates, MRI, Sonography videos, the various 'scopes' like Laparoscopy; Robotic investigations if any. These provide actual information on the location of disease to the doctor. A sub category of Pratyaksh Evidence is called Yukti. This means a typical style of treating a patient as taught by the mentor. This happens in cases of almost all doctors, some give stronger dose first and some at a later stage. This is applying of same medicines but as per differing tradition in different schools of thought.

Let us add that each species has its own speciality with regard to experiencing this world. We know by experience that a dog can identify a thief based on his smell for next three – four months. Here, the smell is a direct evidence for a dog, and humans are using this as inferential knowledge. It is said that female species like cow, goat, she peacocks, she pigeon, mare, etc have similar natural ability to identify poison and the potential danger to life, gifted to them by birth, and we have to explore, experiment and use the same in predictive astrology.

Anumaan PramaaN: Despite increasing scientific advancements in Pratyaksh PramaaN, we see that most of our books go by indirect evidence, called Anumaan PramaaN or inferential wisdom. It has been an age-old and a natural desire for humans to know what is going to happen the next day, the next opportunity, the next benefit etc., and all have been making efforts to somehow know that proverbial 'tomorrow'. No one is an exception to this. Entire world works based on this knowledge, collected and tested for centuries' observations. Let us call this collective knowledge as the unwritten database. This collective wisdom is reflected in traditions established with some variance in different countries. All conclude that it has rained because all streets are so wet; all know that black clouds bring rain; Police suspect that because a person is suddenly found missing, he is likely to be a culprit; a Palash tree has been loaded with new flowers in January, and hence there would be rain after 180 days from then; since sheep are having dysentery, there would be good rains after six days in that area; and we can recall many examples like these in our day to day life.

Be it Ayurved or Allopathy or Homoeopathy, all such methods of treating patients are based on inferential knowledge to a very high degree because it is not always possible to obtain absolutely direct and concrete evidence of any disease. In Ayurved, there are sub chapters in Indriya Shaareer which deal with LakshaNs, available to our 5 Indriya (sensory organs); and also there is chapter on Risht LakshaN (fatal symptoms) which clearly indicate death in different diseases. It would not be wrong to say that over 80% Ayurved or any such science is a set of inferences, drawn based on past observations. In other words, it stipulates that this would happen if these x,y,z conditions are in the background.

As regards Upamaan PramaaN, it is a sub category of Pratyaksh PramaaN as it communicates the fact by giving Similes. Let us see the example of Rabies, the outer symptoms fall in this visual category of Evidence, called Upamaan (simile).

Aapt PramaaN: This is typical to IKS. In this category come the words of wisdom inherited from the wise Sages. Let us understand it by way of an illustration. I recall that as a part of training, I used to assist my Guru Vaidya Dhirendra Bhai Joshi. I was given a table and a chair directly in front of him about 15 feet away. My main job was to take pulse and identify the Naadi, give that sheet to patient before he reached Dhirendra Bhai. It so happened that in one case, when the patient reached him, Dhirendra Bhai started looking at me with shock and anger. Later, I was told that why I failed to hear him while he walked, because when a patient walks with noise of his feet or his shoes, he is generally a patient of Vaayu. Thus, I came to know that there were many things considered as Aapt PramaaN like this. I also recall that in Ayurved, milk of a black cow is a medicine for Vaayu Patients. Like this, there are many things which are honoured because the same are said to be the words of wisdom. While Bhrigu Samhita or any such Samhitaa giving details on predictions based on Horoscopy are believed to be Aapt PramaaN in Astrology; the Samhitaa compiled by scholars like Varah Mihir are considered to be Aapt PramaaN for predicting rain, particularly in Indian subcontinent. Thus, Ayurved adopts Aapt PramaaN.

Charak Rishi, has written more about diagnosis in Indriya Sthaan chapter of his Samhitaa. He has explained how different diseases emanate and how the same can be identified. Charak lists out the signs of a certain Death, and he has given a few illustrations to guide the practitioners. These need to be considered as Aapt PramaaN. He advises that when the inevitable death is on threshold, the prudent doctor should politely change the attitude in favour of Nature: No doctor can ever win over the death; and any effort to show supremacy of Medicine over Nature will bring defame to the Science, and as a result, even treatable patients will lose faith in Life. We see that many hospitals put nearly dead people on Ventilator today; and the image of all hospitals is spoilt.

It is a fact that there are many conditions listed in Ayurved which fall in the category of mental diseases. They may like to treat those conditions by way of drugs. In fact, Ayurved classifies them as mental crimes, and not diseases as such. For example, I may add that Prajyaaparaadh is a major cause of many diseases, mental and physical, which is out of the gamut of modern diagnosis. It belongs to a mental crime of sorts, maybe a breach of moral values and ethics like a theft, covered so skilfully that it always remains undetected! For such disease-like conditions, Ayurved suggests matching remedy of Havan or Mantra or Charity or Praayashchit or a mix of all these. I am just presenting the scope of Ayurved which we are going to connect with the Telegnosis. Though Prajnaaparaadh cannot be brought under modern diagnosis, it is very much a subject traceable under Telegnosis.

A note on influence of Anumaan PramaaN
I know that the economic policies of almost all countries are based on predictions of monsoon or are in anticipation of a normal monsoon. If the rains fail or otherwise, the scenario will change automatically. And that will change rates of interest and GDP, the crop insurance, Share market, and what not! Hence, in the Policy documents, a very tactful mention is made that a normal monsoon is presumed. The words may differ, but the meaning is nothing short of Policy being based on assumptions, either based on data-based machines or by man; but dependence is on prophecy anyway. This is the power of inferential knowledge.

Even the most scientific brains are influenced by such assumption-based affairs. It is not always possible for anyone to use scientific instruments before making his day to day decisions. As a result, even in scientifically advanced countries like England and US, we do not find thirteenth floor in a multi-storeyed building of more than that number! They tried to name Apollo 13, but it really had a technical problem and the astronauts were to be saved. Surprisingly, this is not happening in East where they freely accept number 13 as normal. In Muslim world 786 is respected as an auspicious number. What I want to say is that such traditions do have a history and need to be respected until proved wrong with the same force. How shall I prove 13 as a good omen while 786 is not. In view of such complicated social thinking, we need to make efforts to find out whether we can make use of it for correct decision making! It is, thus, a fact that we follow a golden rule "Peeche dekh, Aage chal" (Walk ahead by looking back). We cannot totally do away with such regional or cultural omens, but I feel that Omens or LakshaNs as obtaining in language of Nature is something different and is far more realistic than such regional omens. Those need to be taken as PramaaN and need to be used to predict or answer the questions as discussed in Telegnosis.

Notes

Preparation for Telegnosis

We have already seen how does an idea or a question arise? It issues from one of the four VaaNi in any live animal. We also know that due to our developed system we are able to produce different vowels and consonants to express our feelings. One of such feelings is a question. We also know that all have a desire to know their future for varying reasons. Hence, humans put questions before foretellers in their own language.

After a question is delivered, it is up to the astrologer to selflessly guide the querist. It is therefore necessary that the question is understood in all possible ways. Sages have devised many methods, some mathematical and some non-mathematical, to understand and answer the question. Under Telegnosis, it is presumed that only genuine questions are respectfully presented before the astrologer, and that the intention is to get guidance. In other words, the questions, asked just for the sake of it or to test the knowledge of astrologer, cannot be answered correctly because those questions are no question in strict sense. In such cases, the querist does not need any guidance.

In India, there was a tradition to respectfully invite or approach the astrologer for seeking his guidance. In other chapters also, we are going to remind the reader that the astrologer has to be extremely observant inasmuch as nothing should miss his attention. Every sound, every change in situation, the smell, etc., should be in his knowledge because every such thing does form a part of answer. Let us coin a term Environmentograph. **He should be able to click an Environmentograph, exactly at the moment when the question is presented to him by the querist. An astrologer has to be an expert Environmentographer.** Correctness of answers will depend on his ability to observe everything around him. This will help him not only in making the Horoscope by using mathematics but will also equip him in assembling the other components of the Answer by using the other nonmathematical methods.

I feel that the following exercises will substantially add to ability of astrologer as a foreteller:-

1. **Naadi Shodhan:** For any spiritual performance, it is expected that one has done Naadi Shodhan. It is a term used in Yog. This refers to a cool state of mental and physical health - as a result of following Rules of Yog. Generally, all adults have accumulated residue, stuck inside the organs, more so in lungs, intestines, arteries etc. It is either removed by appropriate number of Upavaas under supervision of an expert on Ayurved; or by doing Bhasktrikaa PraaNaayaam for appropriate period, say three months. It is said that if one does 120 Bhastrikaa PraaNaayaam for about three months, the body becomes fit enough to start his spiritual journey. Spiritual world does not mean anything like black magic. It, to me, means that the body becomes fit for training on concentration of mind, required for this purpose. It may be added that if one is not able to do Bhastrikaa due to any physical weakness or is not able to devote enough time for Bhastrikaa, the Bhraamari

PraaNaayaam will be good alternative for them - where one is expected to inhale air in a normal way but while exhaling, a humming tone from the place between eyebrows (Aajnaa Chakra) is produced in as low volume as possible, and for as long duration as possible according to age. It must be noted that one should never exert in any PraaNaayaam at any stage, as that can lead to incurable respiratory diseases or irreversible conditions like deafness, eye problems.

2. **Traatak:** For training mind to concentrate on subtle subjects, Traatak is a handy and harmless tool. In this, an effort is made to look at a small red or dark round spot made on a clean White wall for about two hours a day from a comfortable distance where the source of light is from behind us. Some choose to focus eyes on a flame of a lamp, placed in a dark room where other objects are not visible. Here, efforts are made to naturally minimize blinking of eyes. If done at a noiseless place, the concentration will become easy. When one is able to see the spot or the flame even with the closed eyes, the person is said to have received the first basic qualification. As the progress is made, the objects kept outside, start getting corelated with heartbeats felt in the nerves of eyes. Such concentration obviously makes one exceptional in varying ways, and we can say that one is set to extend one's natural capabilities like remote sensing. If we read about Traatak and Naad in Hathayogapradeepika, we are likely to get better insight than said above, but that would be a bonus. Some people prefer to gaze at a red coloured point on a white wall or board from a reasonable distance. Some keep watching the full Moon. The impact is similar and mental faculties start becoming trained and

the saadhak is able to sense or interpret or scan the surroundings much better every day. I recall of a discussion
of Osho with my friend Shri Dinkar Bhai Jani at Dhandhuka Post Office, where Osho, on being asked about his
exceptionally powerful eyes, said that his Traatak had
enabled him to see clearly the filament of a light of a
running truck in the dark night! I have personally heard
Baapaa (an Amreli based MBBS, turned a Sanyasi) saying that due to Traatak, the running water of Ganga boils
around the feet of Saadhak while doing Soorya traatak
(Traatak done on midday Sun). It is advised that in the
initial period, one should stop traatak when eyes fill up
with water. The duration should be increased gradually,
and never at the cost of ease.

A person becomes capable of taking note of the external
surroundings and the internal state of mind with regard
to visuals and the sounds. As the progress is made, we
start receiving the signals as to what could be the most
probable meaning of the constant changes in the environment around us. One gradually starts realizing that
the sounds and visuals change and that each change is an
independent communication. This is what is called language of animals and plants and also the connotations
made by each non-living object within the eye-sight or
earshot. This helps Telegnosis when read with reference
to a clear question.

3. **Naad Shravan:** In this method, the person is required to
    sit for long hours, and try to hear the sound of his own
    body which becomes more and more clear over a period
    of time. In the initial stage, one keeps ears pressed to hear
    the sound inside one's own body! Better if Shaambhavee

Mudra is done under guidance of a qualified Yogi. All Naath Gurus, Guru Naanak and many others have recommended this technique to train mind of Saadhak. Similar Saadhanaa is recommended in Pushti sampradaay. In Hathayogapradeepika, Naad is said to be having four different frequencies like bell, thunder, guitar and flute. In other books, a sound of roaring sea is also mentioned. The objective, here, is to concentrate on the sound, heard inside our body. Over a period of time, no wonder that one can hear the sounds occurring far away, and the ones coming from a thousand miles in advanced stage of meditation! It will not be wrong if we say that Naad Shravan is one type of Traatak. This can be done during day time also, unlike Traatak which is generally done in dark places. It will be helpful to refer to wonderful books like Hathayogapradeepika for fine details. When we feel that we are able to receive signals of future happening, we can stop the Saadhanaa. That will be enough for Telegnosis.

4. **Prism Gazing:** This refers to a practise to observe the spectrums of objects, kept on the other side of a prism. I have written about respected Shri Joshi of Rajkot who is able to see the Chhaayaa or aura of a person and predict about his state of mind or likelihood of a disease in near future. In Jain philosophy, a term Leshyaa is used which is very close to this concept. It is said that to a trained eye, the past deeds are as much visible like an object, called Leshyaa, which get reflected in one's Aura. Based on that, prediction can be made at least about his health in near future. In some special way, this comes in the category of Traatak that can provide detailed information of physical and mental position of any living being.

Logically, a spectrum of a dead animal does differ from that of a living animal, and based on such colour variations, the birds like vultures, decide whether to descend on a prey or not. A champion of so many sciences, including prism gazing, correctly said that there has to be a notable difference between colour spectrum of a Radio set when it is on, and when it is put off; similarly he highlights that how spectrum should differ when a person is ill or angry, and certainly before he is going to fall ill; and he says it is for this reason that a hungry fly does not rush to photograph of banana, even when it is taken by a very high resolution camera! This is so because all animals have this faculty to scan the surrounding environment with regard to smell, touch, taste, appearance etc. We, humans, also can grossly identify a dead body of an animal lying in the field quite far from us. He says that everyone has that ability to sense, and it can be scaled up by Prism gazing. Chhaayaa clearly shows anger, disease, peace of mind, and Prism gazing trains our eye to see the same around body of all.

In relevant chapters, Ayurved has reference to change in Chhaayaa and Pratichhaayaa of a patient according to Tridosh and also due to improvement in his condition or otherwise. We shall see those aspects in the other chapter.

Svami Jagannath Teerth writes that a Yogi can extend or expand his Chhaayaa as per his needs, and everything in that area becomes knowledge of the yogi. My limited experiments tell that to be true in some cases. It, therefore, is good to keep this in back of mind while answering questions.

5. **Jap :** This is another harmless way to train the brain. The Guru asks his disciple to create a specific frequency of sound inside his mind, preferably without lip movement. This activates the centres inside his brain to spark the spiritual progress. It is said that the lower the volume of Jap, better is the impact. Good examples are given; the horn of a diesel railway engine is more clearly heard from a long distance; and the dog whistle or a thunder whistle that are not at all heard by human ear but do create communicative channels.

6. **Praayashchit:** However good a Saadhak may be, there are actions in everyone's life for which he feels responsible and guilty too; and wishes that those actions were not taken by him. In the West, the Church has built a Confession Box for this purpose, but the Medicine Men in the West are yet to treat Confession Box as a part of medical treatment. In India, this is considered an essential part of daily routine and also at all the religious functions. This enables Saadhak to come out clean and attain required concentration of mind. Ayurved recognized this as a remedy.

7. **TarpaN :** TarpaN has proved to be the most effective tool not only for mental relief, but also as a tool to communicate with the invisible and inaudible souls around us with continuous and dedicated practise. This does liberate many unsatiated souls, if done selflessly, and therefore increases chances of attaining good spiritual progress in less time than taken by a normal Saadhak. TarpaN means offering potable water to the dead persons and animals, daily. Water is slowly poured on earth from a glass to quench their thirst, their unfulfilled desires, and with a

request to forgive for any untoward incident. It is also a prayer to the God to liberate those souls. I have seen thousands of people benefit from TarpaN. For the sake of argument, it is said that based on what concrete evidence do the scientists disprove the existence of invisible souls around us? We cannot say that Aakaash is as empty as it appears to be, if there are invisible dust particles, it does have invisible souls too. Let us remember that though no electrical engineers have seen electricity, and no atomic scientists have seen an atom; and still we know that these are the facts. It may not be possible to answer questions that are asked to tease a Saadhak.

Notes

Jyotish & Astrology

Whether in East or in West, the concept of the Sky (considered of 360 degree) and Orbits of Sun and Earth is the same. Both schools divide Sky in 12 Raashi (Signs) and 27 Nakshatr (Constellations). Thus, one Raashi gets 30 degrees; and one constellation gets 13.33 degrees. The latter is finer than the former, but it is the matter of individual's choice. Both schools consider nine planets as main indicators of events, past or future.

Horoscopy is all about drawing a birth chart at the time of birth of a person (or any animal), and placing the major planets Sun, Moon, Mars, Venus, Mercury, Jupiter and Saturn; (also, Rahu and Ketu which are nothing but two imaginary reference points that divide the orbit into two equal parts in the Sky) to be placed in the twelve Houses, representing almost all aspects of life. The first House shows the Raashi that was rising on the East horizon at the time of birth or question, as the case may be. People who study this in further detail, concentrate on the Constellation in that Raashi that was rising on East horizon. This enables astrologers to accordingly visualize positions of planets and make a prediction in the light of their aggregate impact. Such foretelling of longevity and important events of a person is called Natal Horoscopy or life reading. In every horoscope, movement of planets and Houses is considered from Left to Right, which is the movement of Earth around its axis.

Some hold a view that Jyotish is the correct term to indicate predictive Astrology. Jyotish is related to word Jyoti, or a lamp – presumably in the dark universe. A lamp can only show little area around it, and we can take advantage of that light to safeguard our interests. The fact remains that this small lamp cannot fight the infinite darkness, and fear of every unknown factor hidden there. In other words, predictive astrology, **Telegnosis, shows opportunities available around us at that particular time; but not in unlimited light as generally expected.**

With regard to predictive astrology, it is said that the Kundali (Chart) shows what we are supposed to face as a result of our Praarabdh: It is presumed that we have most probably 'faced' all our Sanchit Karm before our present birth either in the heaven or hell, proverbial or factual. Hence, the planets in the Chart are nothing but a map of how we are going to face our Praarabdh Karm in this birth. The planets, placed in any Kundali, therefore only indicate the events, and do not cause the events. Common people are under impression that planets cause events, and many astrologers also believe that due to lack of scientific knowledge and logic. It is for such reasons that Saints like Svami Dayanand Sarasvati have said that pooja or pacification of Mangal, Shani etc., is not in accordance with Ved, and that Jyotish was never considered Eye of Ved, in this context. For predictive astrology, it is safe to say that this is the art of interpretation and drawing an inference, because everything is considered to be a LakshaN of some other thing: It is all about decoding symbols. Many find this not readily acceptable, and perhaps they are not prepared to do any research. For common people, it is not logical that Solar eclipse is followed by Lunar eclipse, but for students of Astronomy, it has to happen; and can be predicted very exactly. One of my colleagues, also a post graduate in modern education system, shocked me by saying that the 'Eclipse will be seen tomorrow only if the Supreme God allows'! Let us not allow such people to stop us from learning the mathematics behind Jyotish (Khagol or astronomy).

If we do not add Numerology and Palmistry, Jyotish has six branches. Jaatak means the life reading based on Lagn at the time of birth. Gol refers to knowing current position of planets, or spherical astronomy. Nimitta (LakshaN) means the omens supporting the predictive conclusions. Prashn Jyotish means answering specific questions based on the time of question. Muhoort means finding the most beneficial time for a desired event, in West they call it Electional Astrology. GaNit refers to Mathematical astronomy to know eclipse etc., and GaNit is also applied for working out 16 types of sub charts (often known as D charts like Hora, Navamaansh, Dvaadashaansh Kundali), which are all based on the birth chart and from these charts specific features like Happiness, Family, Education, Character, Marriage are studied. Chapter 18 of Prashn Marg has included some special entirely new features like Nav Navamaansh and Navaansh Dvaadashaansh to dig deep into future. There are two methods of calculating Dashaa viz., Vinshottari and Ashtottari Dashaa. In each of these, they calculate, Antaradasha and Pratyantaradashaa etc. On predictive astrology, we find Samhitaas (edited works) of great sages like Bhrigu, Varah Mihir, Paaraashar, Vasisht, Atri, Chyavan, Yavan and many more. Thus, at present, we have eight branches of Predictive Astrology on hand. We must remember that astrology is not mathematics, otherwise all mathematicians would have been excellent astrologers. Let us agree that India has always admitted new evidence in its fold of knowledge, and maybe tomorrow, new sciences like Graphology will also form part of predictive astrology.

Based on types of questions put before the astrologers, horary astrology covers Electional Astrology or Muhoort, Nasht Prashn (when astrologer is expected to read the mind of querist), Koop Prashn (locating a well), Krushi Prashn (about farming operations), Santati or Santaan Prashn (about the children), Garbh Prashn (about pregnancy), Bhojan Prashn (what food was ingested), Surati Prashn (making physical love), Mrugayaa Prashn (king asking about his success in hunting game), Vivaah Prashn (about marriage proposals), Daiv Prashn (about temples), Varshaa or Parjanya Prashn (About rains), Svaasthya Prashn (about health), Chourya Prashn (about the theft). These are the major areas of concern. We continue to receive questions regarding these subjects even today. Of course, some new subjects like going to foreign countries for education and marriage, getting Visa, lottery tickets, etc., are a few new additions where guidance of astrologers is requested.

Man is an untiring animal and is still making efforts to convert unfavourable situations into the most convenient opportunity. For this reason, we find references to remedial situations in the form of magic and use of herbs (generally in Atharv Ved). Some have rejected Atharv Ved by stamping it as for the people who are not so sophisticated. Magic is called as Yaatu, and with a rather negative interpretation of this term. The Left and the West have branded Bhaaratiya philosophy as full of black magic, and therefore backward, though only a very small part of Atharv Ved speaks of these in a tone of prayers for the overall good of all. It is largely so because the history is always written by the Ruler, and they ruled India for over two hundred years. They wrote whatever they wanted to implant an inferiority complex in our minds, and they seem to be successful in doing that. The main reason is that they had monopoly as far as printing machines and modern technology are concerned. They made available whatever reading and visual material they decided, and no one had that power. But it does not mean that whatever was printed and presented by them was a truth beyond doubt. Slowly Indian Knowledge Systems are getting equipped to provide concrete historical proof in a befitting language to convince the World that the fact was otherwise.

The propaganda that concept of Zero did not originate in India is illogical when we read Chapter 17 of Yajurved which states how we can count numbers in decimal system. It is added that Yajurved, by any means, is certainly older than Roman Civilisation or Egyptian Culture. Calculations involved in Astronomy relating to important events like Eclipse, did need mathematical systems and this decimal system was the most popular. It is said that system of calculating things with Six as the unit was also in existence, but I do not have elaborate information about this.

We have already read everything about how different units of Time were used in Vedic era, and how the words like Muhoort and Hora came into existence. We know that due to Hora, the modern world measures time in minute, day, week, month, year; and like that. We know who brought the uniformity in sequence of weekdays, and how logically!

We need to know that Astrology, more with reference to Astronomy, is called the Eye of Vedas. To say the least, this means that we certainly knew those celestial movements much better, and that too more based on our intellectual ability than the telescopes. It is difficult to imagine how intelligent they were. Based on the varying celestial positions, they wrote their inferences for each season, for each major agricultural crop, for medicinal plants, for ideal time and lunar date to travel (e.g., with reference to tide and ebb), for performing Yajn (medicated smoke) as well as hymns, addressed in praise of divine givers called Devata like Varun (as Water), Vayu (for Wind), Agni (the form changing factor), Soorya (as centre of this solar system), Moon (leading to seasons and climatic changes and mental status and menstrual cycles among female species). Many examples can be cited. In a nutshell, by inducting a sense of worship in every walk of life, the entire civilization was taught to protect the environment; and that everyone was educated to respect everything. Every heart was made to become constantly thankful and blissful.

Notes

Jyotish & Horary

As said above, Jyotish (more as an astronomical calculation) is called Eye of Ved and is generally used for performing various types of Yajn on a specific Tithi, date and time - based on changing angle between Sun and Moon. In Tantra, the Anushthaan are generally taken up from Shukla Pratipadaa. Further, in Tantra, a Yajn seems to be more goal oriented as against a Vedic Yajn. Vedic events are more like thanks-giving process. Therefore, in Tantra, the horoscopy has more room where a person can ask as to when he should start a result-oriented anushthaan e.g., to please a specific deity!

This brings before us the fact that human mind has always had an instinct to know that by doing what he would stand benefited in a given situation. He has been willing to do everything to attain his goals, and for that purpose he resorts to Astrology – as it is the oldest tool to look into the unknown future. The same inquisitiveness has resulted in invention of a satellite. We expect it to tell that when clouds are likely to reach us so that we can plan our schedule accordingly, but during those days, farmers heavily depended on astrologers. It is logical to think that predictive astrology commenced with questions relating Rains. Varah Mihir and many others have written in Sanskrit about when to expect rains, based on (i) position of planets, and (ii) movements of living beings around us. Generally, these predictions of rain were relevant for an area within a radius of five miles. We also have similar literature in local languages written by Bhadali and Ghaag, which is relevant to the western coast of India! Thus, we see that the tendency to foresee events, like rains, has remained same whether we do it by using Sanskrit Shlok of wizards like Varah Mihir, or by following Bhadali Vaakya or by using satellite images! The human mind continues to be equally or perhaps more eager to know about his tomorrow.

In the West, **Electional Astrology is a branch which is close to Telegnosis.** Electional Astrology involves drawing a horary/ Prashn chart to decide the best time to start a particular work called MEP (Most Effective Point) and does not take into consideration the other branches which we included in India. Decumbiture Chart is again nothing but a chart to know about patient's sickness and longevity. It is nothing but an application of Hellenistic Astrology. In India, astrology is used in many more ways, and we shall see the same in separate chapters.

Horary astrology generally refers to Horoscopy which is a method of answering specific questions based on an Astrological Chart. This is yet another application of chart based Astrology, like the birth charts, where astrologers give their reading of the entire life of the person! Both volumes of Prashn Marg, written by Harihar of Keral, provide elaborate information on Horary astrology. The commentary written by Pt. B V Raman is without a parallel. Of course, such subjects were also covered in many PuraaN in Bhaarat, but Prashn Marg is like a ready reckoner. It is felt that we have failed to make use of such elaborate knowledge already available in our books. Let us start working on it anew, at least for forming second opinions - before taking the final action in any sphere of modern life. It can immediately pay its dividend if applied in medical diagnosis which is becoming more and more accurate but is also becoming increasingly unaffordable for the most!

Similarly, crimes are increasing fast to ensure a comparable lifestyle, inspired by consumerism. The modern states are too democratic in administration. As a result, the Police and Judiciary are not able to effectively cope up with the crimes! It is felt that if Telegnosis is adopted, particularly in the fields of crime detection and interrogations, the society will stand benefitted in terms of time and cost both. We can introduce Telegnostic skills between FIR and Charge sheet, at least as a second opinion or supporting method.

We are going to deal with most aspects of Horary Astrology in this compilation. On a careful study of ancient books, it is felt that there was a system in India where the astrologers were respectfully invited by people at home for seeking guidance about some real social issues. Astrologers were taught to give correct answers without prejudice. They never took up wasteful challenges to answer questions just for the sake of it. The astrologers were supposed to be leading a very spiritual and simple life without financial reward from fellow citizens. In modern days, the system has changed, and astrologers have opened offices where they give the advice for a fee, just like a doctor or a lawyer. In old days, the astrologer had good scope to rely on the LakshaN (omens) on the way, which is not possible now because most astrologers have opened offices where the querists are expected to come. But I feel that since every time, there is a change in querist, his belongings, his clothes, gestures, the external happenings like on the road outside the office etc., a vigilant astrologer still can function without any problems being seated in his office. It needs to be noted that Telegnosis expects exceptional ability to read what we can say an Environmentograph. This is something in addition to his knowledge of drawing a natal horoscope, be that with help of a computer or otherwise. We are going to elaborate what we mean by this term Environmentograph, when we have discussed various predictive methods. A few methods are nonmathematical and will be largely new for many – especially finding the Aaroodh Lagn and ascertaining strength of Bhaav.

Notes

Draw a Kundali or Horoscope (Chart)

Horary astrology, sometimes known as Electional astrology, is the most popular, and the oldest form of foretelling, which exists in all civilizations. In some countries, Solar systems are prevalent, while in India, Lunar or even Nakshatra (Constellation) based calculations are practiced. The literature on this subject is such huge that we cannot deal with all finer aspects, hence, we will briefly cover only those aspects that matter for answering the genuine questions, expressly presented before the astrologer for seeking help. As said elsewhere, only genuine questions are to be considered as questions, and for this reason, no answer is possible to questions which are outside that definition. There is a difference of opinion on this issue. Some believe that all deserve astrological guidance – whether they present the question or not; and vice versa. But I side with the school of thought that expects a question to be so presented for guidance. Unless there is a question, there cannot be an answer, how there can be!

Drawing a birth chart is the most common branch of Astrology across the world. In a nutshell, this is an effort to know which Raashi is rising on the East horizon at the time of birth of a person or at the time of question. This requires knowledge of mathematics to know or calculate the relative position of the other stars in the sky and place them in the

Kundali. The Raashi, rising on East Horizon, to that degree, is called as the Lagn or Ascendant which is considered as the first House, of the twelve Houses of any Kundali. Horoscope is the English word for Kundali. Because it was drawn in a Kundal, a circular diagram, in the ancient time, it is called Kundali. Still in many parts of India, it is drawn in that form. However, a rectangular form is also equally popular. The movement of planets within the Kundali is always from left to right, and the Houses are also numbered in that way.

In Telegnosis, we are concerned with answering a question without lengthy calculations etc., and for that reason, we need to adopt the short cuts to draw, and analyse the Kundali. Generally, Almanac is used to accurately construct the Kundali, but that may not be always possible for an astrologer, sitting in a remote area or while travelling to certain places. Further, in many cases, the querist brings his birth chart etc., and presents the same for reading. In such cases, we need to know the short cuts to verify whether the Chart is correct or not. Astrologer should not base his predictions on an incorrect Chart.

Let us see what the masters like Harihar say about Aaroodh. From him, we learn that it is always advisable that predictions are based on Aaroodh or Prashn Lagn, supported by nonmathematical methods. He, thus, gives secondary place even to the birth chart about Horary astrology. He also insists that immediately after the Aaroodh is found out, astrologer should keep noting all LakshaN around him. In that environment, everything forms part of answer. There are some school specific methods to find out Aaroodh. We shall discuss the methods in this chapter.

Today, astrologers do not go on visit and almost everything around them in that office is static, but the principles of Telegnosis still apply because, the time, the omen, the querist, number of visitors, their dress, discussions etc., change every time. Further, this method of Aaroodh Lagn becomes useful when the querist cannot speak for any reason, e.g., when his mouth is injured or cannot speak in language that the astrologer can understand! It is always expected that the astrologer will start from his residence at the most appropriate and good time and will not be missing any message conveyed by anything, any sound, any discussion, any smell, his own Svar etc., till he is seated in the residence of the querist. He, then, is expected to note the internal ambiance of the house, the directions, articles, sounds, smell, language, number of people, objects and pictures on the walls, people's dress and positions; his own Svar (side of breath) etc. It is believed that nothing in the life occurs without any reason, and astrologers are required to note and corelate every such thing with the question put before him because the answer is hidden in those things.

In a Kundali, particularly in Horary astrology, the Bhaav are perhaps more important than the position of planets. One will appreciate how excellently and expertly the Sages have assigned everything to these twelve Houses. This only makes the interpretation possible, but due to a lot of symbolism involved, everything is debatable. Experience will however prove that Sages were right at every step.

Method (Based on Sun's position)
Many a time, a question is asked to an astrologer, seated in mountain/ forest/ during travel etc., and neither he, nor the querist knows the Raashi of Moon at that time. In such situ-

ations, a non-traditional approach is to be adopted. A blank horoscope is to be made in soil as said above, and astrologer should note the place (Bhaav) touched by the querist. After that, the astrologer should place Sun as per the time of question (as indicated in table given below in this chapter).

Sometimes querists bring with them their birth chart etc. and produce the same for ready reference. When a birth chart is presented before an astrologer, it is advisable to crosscheck it quickly as to its being correct. We are discussing a thumb rule for this, which is not very fine calculation, but still is dependable irrespective of place of birth place. The blank chart is divided in two vertical halves, the right half stands for the day and the left one represents dark half. Each house is allotted two hours. These are also called as Visible/ Bright Half and Invisible/ Dark Half. The first house is given time of morning 6 to 8 O clock. Since first and seventh house are divided in equal halves (half dark and half bright), the left portion of the first house represents 6 to 7 a.m.; and the right portion of the seventh house stands for 6 to 7 p.m., respectively. The planets in dark half are generally believed to be less powerful and therefore they give delayed results or reduced results as compared to the ones posited in bright half.

Now, please take a look at the table given below. Suppose, X is born at 3 p.m., Sun should be placed in ninth House. If it is not so, the birth chart would be most probably wrong, making all subsequent predictions questionable. In such cases, it is better to depend on Horary chart, to be prepared based on the time of question.

Let us say if the time is 9 a.m., the sun will be in the House number 12; and accordingly, all planets, then, can be placed, if Almanac becomes available. To understand this better, let us think that the question was asked on 18 January, the Sun is in Makar at 2 degrees. This, therefore, will lead to Kumbh Lagn (also of less than 5 degrees). The other planets then should be placed as per Almanac or the from the newspapers. We know that most of the periodicals publish detailed position of each star in their daily editions. This, being based on movement of Sun, is easy to construct more so because generally all know the month and day of question. We have found this method to be working well at any time.

This is a short cut to make any birth chart or any Horary chart. This is a crude method but has been of immense use in my own experience. Position of Sun should be as shown in the table below in any correct Kundali. The process is simple, first note the time of question, then get a blank Chart drawn by the querist; and place Sun as shown in the table given below:-

Sr. No.	House where Sun will be	Time of question / Sun in Birth Chart	Dark or Bright Half
1	1st House	Between 6 and 8 am	Half Dark & Half Bright
2	2nd House	Between 4 & 6 AM	Invisible
3	3rd House	Between 2 & 4 AM	Invisible
4	4th House	Between 12 & 2 AM	Invisible
5	5th House	Between 10 &12 PM	Invisible
6	6th House	Between 8 & 10 PM	Invisible
7	7th House	Between 6 & 8 PM	Visible
8	8th House	Between 4 & 6 PM	Visible

9	9th House	Between 2 & 4 PM	Visible
10	10th House	Between 12 & 2 PM	Visible
11	11th House	Between 10 & 12 AM	Visible
12	12th House	Between 8 & 10 AM	Visible

Let it be added that from Lagn to 6th House is called the Invisible Half and it is believed that the planets, posited there show substantial impact during the life time while the planets, posited from 7th to 12th House show impact either in late life or the results are reduced drastically. This, in this illustration, will make Sun Lord Ascendant in 4th House in Invisible Half. This means that Sun, with regard to Prashn Kundali, will show slow impact in coming days and the impact will be reduced. Astrology is all about art of interpretation of such contradictory-looking observations.

The following table will tell where the Sun should be posited (it is presumed that all know that Sun enters Makar on every 15 January and stays in each Raashi for 30 days in an anti-clockwise movement inside Kundali i.e., it will enter Kumbh on 15 February):-

Sr. No.	House where Sun will be	Sun enters on
1	Makar	15 January
2	Kumbh	15 February
3	Meen	15 March
4	Mesh	15 April
5	Vrushabh	15 May
6	Mithun	15 June

7	Kark	15 July
8	Simh	15 August
9	Kanyaa	15 September
10	Tulaa	15 October
11	Vrushchik	15 November
12	Dhanu	15 December

Such will be the position of Sun in a Kundali, and this is how we can crosscheck the veracity of a readymade Kundali. This is a good and a quick tool to know whether a given Kundali is prima facie correct.

Illustration of this Solar method

Let us construct a trial chart now with just this much known to us. Suppose, a question is asked at 1 AM on 20 January. As per the first table, Sun should be in 4th House; and as per the second table, Sun will be in Makar Raashi, approx. 5 degree. Hence let us put Sun in forth House, write the number 10 (Makar Raashi) there, and number all the Houses anticlockwise. We get Tulaa Lagn. Since the Sun is about 5 degree, it is to be treated as Baal Avasthaa (a stage where a person cannot express his feelings, capacity, ability etc., with clarity). Further, the Sun is posited in the visible half which shows bright possibilities of quick results. Once we consider the following feature, our first opinion will be ready:

- The impact of Sun being in House of Shani, not good!
- The impact in the fourth House!
- Sun is posited in the Invisible Half.
- Lord of Lagn-Kundali is Mangal!
- Let us place Moon if the Lunar date is known.

Generally, all these things, including the current position of all planets, are available from daily newspapers or on

WhatsApp groups. Let us see a quick analysis for Telegnosis. Note that we will consider planets up to 10 degrees as Baal, between 11 and 20 degree as young and expressive; and between 21 and 30 degrees, the planet should be considered as weak but mature. This concept should be kept in the back of mind for inter se interpretation, when necessary.

It will be appropriate to add here that in any Kundali, interpretation with regard to connection between these 12 Houses is also required. In other words, each house is typically connected with the remaining houses as a unit: suppose we want to know about heart (nature) and mother of A, we will immediately study the 4th House, but when we are asked to tell something related with his maternal grandmother, we should take that 4th House as first and study the 4th from there. Thus, the maternal grandmother of A (mother of A's mother) is represented by 7th House in A's birth chart. Similarly, his paternal grandmother will be seen from 4th House from 10th House which is A's own house or the Lagn itself! The explanation of this principle can run in huge volume hence, it is better to learn this logic of inter se connection of these 12 Houses/ Bhaav. Let us add one more example before proceeding further. B is younger brother of A, so he will be studied from 3rd House in A's kundali; and B's wife will be studied from 9th House (7th House from 3rd House) in A's kundali.

Let us be mindful of the fact that we expect astrologer to be always able to hear and see the surrounding without missing anything at all. About all methods in this chapter, we propose to show how the astrologer would be ready with the Aaroodh or Lagn Kundali in one of these ways, and we will present broad features of what is meant by position of Sun and Moon in the Horary astrology as being discussed here. Here, we will also give a unique way to ascertained strength or otherwise of each Bhaav.

Nonmathematical methods - Horary Astrology – Aaroodh (Prashn Kundali – Janm Lagn Kundali)

Let us see nonmathematical way of calculating the Lagn or Ascendant. Harihar, as elaborated by Hon'ble Shri B.V.Raman, explains Aaroodh Lagn. There it is stated (Chapter 9/32) that only when for some reasons, astrologer is not able to decide Aaroodh, he should go for drawing chart based on the other (traditional) methods. Readers can find that wonderful account for exact interpretation, but I am simplifying based on my own experience. In my experience, Aaroodh Lagn is related to the direction where querist has preferred to be seated or has preferred to stand at the place of meeting; while Aaroodh Raashi is the Bhaav where the querist touches with his hand or places an object. Aaroodh Lagn is recommended at many places in Prashn Marg as it is more natural as compared with mathematical astrological systems. The querist himself indicates at Aaroodh Lagn. **It is called Aaroodh because it deals with the idea, riding the mind of the querist.** I have seen that this is more in tune with the Nature. Any words would fall short to thank Shri Harihar and Shri Raman for unravelling this secret which is so handy but is too inexplicable for a layman, unless tried; and I have tried it successfully. I have dropped the concept of an object made of gold etc., because it is not practicable, today. Sometimes, I even make a mental Horoscope either on a table or a plain paper, or a piece of land etc., and ask the questioner to identify his place of choice; and note the Lagn.

Method 1

The querist is shown a horoscope diagram and is asked to draw a blank horoscope on a clean piece of paper. Then he is required to touch any part of the diagram. Astrologer, then, should mark that House (that Bhaav) as Aaroodh or Raashi Kundali based on Moon. The way this blank horoscope (clockwise or otherwise, with or without broken lines etc.) is drawn represents the balance Karm of the querist. He may inadvertently make some houses incomplete, some extended; some lines will be broken, some houses will be open on the borders and like that. Astrologer should place Moon there and write down the Raashi occupied by Moon at that time. This will be followed by placing all other planets as available in Almanac. For this, the astrologer should know the position of Moon at that time. It is seen that generally the querist touches the Bhaav which are abnormal in size and shape. Suppose, Moon is in Mesh at that hour, the querist touches 12th House which becomes Aaroodh Raashi. Hence, Moon will be placed there. This will make a Kundali of Vrushabh Lagn. In place of piece of paper, querist can be asked to make it with his finger on a good, clean and levelled place of land. If the querist can draw the rough diagram of a blank horoscope, importance will also be given to the direction in which he draws the first lines, and how he plans this drawing. As said elsewhere, the lines drawn by querist and the Houses so drawn by him will show the strength of those respective Bhaav. In this case, since the querist has touched 12th House, more importance should be given to lines and contours of that part. It is important to note the order in which the blank horoscope was drawn: If line is first drawn in East or North, predict good; if West, the problem may worsen; and if South, death or sad end of the project is to be predicted. A clockwise drawing is considered good, and vice versa. When the horoscope is well drawn, it is indicative of overall good, and wherever the lines are faint, inside the chart or on borders, the strength is understood to be lacking; and wherever the lines are broken, astrologer should predict delay or leakage, lack of support or failure. Broken lines, inside the horoscope results into connecting any two or more Houses, and accordingly the predictions need to be made.

Method 2

A unique and surprising method is also included in Prashn Marg, which we find to be working very well. Suppose astrologer is faced with a situation where the querist is unable to speak or express his question, verbally or non-verbally, for some reason, in such a situation the astrologer should consider the Aaroodh based on where the querist is looking. He should note that who, in that gathering is the querist and where he was looking when the matter of asking a question came up; or what was the direction that he occupied when the matter came up. Here, the position of querist is decided with astrologer being the reference point, in other words, position of querist is to be noted from the place where astrologer is seated, as if astrologer is in the centre of the horoscope. Any change in situation later, may mutilate the answer to a certain extent, and should be ignored. It is added that we can adopt a strategy that when the querist is seated we can take that direction as Ascendant but when the querist is not taking a seat for any reason, the direction in which he is looking at the very time of putting his question is to be taken as the Aaroodh Ascendant.

Sages, as said above, surprisingly assigned eight directions to each of the twelve Raashi in a clockwise manner. This starts from Mesh to Meen and looks diagonally opposite to the traditional astrology; but when experienced, it is seen that it is very pertinent while answering questions. Harihar, in Chapter 2, 17 and 18 of Prashn Marg, has given details of how Aaroodh is worked out and that how it is equal to Lagn Kundali! It is said that with reference to Aaroodh, the clockwise pattern, as said above, is adopted. Suppose the querist is looking in Vaayavya (North West), the sign allotted is Dhanu Raashi. Hence the Aaroodh Lagn will be Dhanu, and all planets will be placed according to Almanac.

Raashi	Direction
Mesh Vrushabh	East
Mithun	Agni
Kark Simh	South
Kanyaa	Nairutya
Tulaa Vrushchik	West
Dhanu	Vaayavya
Makar Kumbh	North
Meen	Ishaanya

Harihar says that astrologer should see from which direction the querist starts drawing the blank chart, whether he made it clockwise, anticlockwise, or with confusion, or drew in a zigzag manner, whether the lines are broken, whether the houses are left uneven and open in any direction! If drawn in soil, where the lines are raised or depressed, what material is prominent in which line and in which house! I have been able to use this method in villages of Bengal where we did not have blank papers.

Let us stop for a second and note one distinguishing feature.

Horoscopy and Horary are two separate branches though they look very similar and often follow same styles of calculations. In Horary astrology, it is presumed that the querist or the Prashn Purush is standing face to face with the astrologer, hence what is on North side of astrologer falls in South for the querist. For this reason, the reader may get confused when the Prashn Marg says that Kark Lagn is to be predicted when the querist is seated or is looking in South direction. The entire Horary astrology is querist-centric. Similar pattern from East, SE, South to NE is also advised referred to in Chapter 28 of famous work Bhuvan Deepika where it is discussed in light of a compilation known as Jinendramaalaa, which could be a book compiled by some Jain scholar: There Vrushabh is assigned to south, Simh to SE, and Meen to NE. After the querist has pointed out the House of his choice, astrologer has two choices. First, he should place Sun in the blank Kundali as per the Table given above and construct the chart; or he should place Moon in the Bhaav (that the querist selected) and construct the Chart. In my opinion, placing of Sun as per Table is more correct; but utmost importance is to be given to the Bhaav where the querist has shown his choice (he should also be asked to select a Bhaav from a blank chart as part of this process). The problem would be invariably related to that House, and the Sun (and Moon etc.) will tell us much more. Success increases with participation of questioner. Many may feel that how without detailed information on each planet, this may work! But these are time-tested methods obtaining in our old books and do work well. In these methods, a deep understanding of Lagn and the twelve Bhaav is of utmost importance, which takes years of experience. Harihar has also shown how the strength of each Bhaav is to be easily interpreted which otherwise, is impossible without arithmetical calculations!

Ascertaining the strength of Bhaav or House

It is necessary to test whether our reading of Bhaav, if done mathematically, is confirmed by the other nonmathematical methods of ascertaining strength or otherwise of Bhaav. For this, for years, I have been using a typical method which is nothing but my extension of what Harihar has advised. Astrologer knows that what is the Aaroodh Lagn, what is the Bhaav chosen by querist, where Sun will be placed as per time of question, and he knows the position of Moon also. Hence, it becomes necessary to interpret that Bhaav, that is the place where he placed his hand or that he indicated somehow. For this, I have been successfully using newspaper cuttings, cloth pieces, used match sticks, small wooden pieces etc. in the place of 12 Betel leaves as detailed in second volume of Prashn Marg. I, therefore, suggest that the querist may be requested to randomly make about 20 pieces of different shapes from any rough or old newspaper or make that many pieces of a long thin tree branch or break some of the match sticks from a matchbox (which is invariably available even in small villages). These paper-pieces, then, should be numbered and received in the way they are given. Suppose, one paper cutting is given with a photo of boy facing the querist, it should be received and placed in the same way. In other words, the photo should still face the giver. If possible, write serial number on it for a reference later. Let us put the first as Lagn, second as the second house, and like that we will have all 12 Houses filled with either these paper-cuttings or with pieces of twig etc. After receiving all twelve, ask querist to pocket the rest of the pieces to avoid confusion. I am glad to record that almost in all such cases, I have found correct presentations of each Bhaav with reference to the questions. Every piece contributed to the answer. The Bhaav, where he originally placed his hand, automatically gets reflected in appropriate size, indicating possibility or otherwise of a success. Thus, we know the strength of each house within two minutes. This is to confirm whether our analysis is not going in wrong direction. It is the easiest crosschecking method I have ever learnt: It is like a Spelling check facility in modern computer machines. The reader may find it interesting that many times, the write up available on those pieces provide answers, and solutions! Once we have calculated Ascendant like this, and studied its importance as said above, it is necessary that we assess power of individual Houses. In normal astrology, the power of each house is assessed by noting which planets aspect it, and if yes, from which house; and whether that aspect is a strong factor considering other planetary positions! And I have always found it to be a lengthy process, clumsy as well. But the above methods themselves surprisingly tell us of the strength or otherwise of each Bhaav, in a very pictorial way. The foregoing makes the following steps:-

- Make the questioner draw a blank horoscope either on a paper or in soil or a table.
- Ask him to touch any part of that horoscope to know Aaroodh as said above.
- Take a mental picture of a horoscope at the place of meeting, and 12 houses.
- Give a newspaper etc. and ask questioner to make about 20 pieces at random, and accept from him 12 pieces, the way he gives. Receive these pieces the way he gives, and do not rearrange the same. Keep writing down the number of the house.
- Sometime give a thin wooden stick like we have in broomstick, and ask him to make about 20 pieces, and accept 12 (if paper pieces are not properly torn). These pieces could be used like paper-cuttings.
- If the horoscope is drawn in soil, I study the size and type

of contours of each House, presence of stones and such other things in each place. Similar study becomes possible based on size, shape, colour (and words if printed on paper) that represent the 12 Houses in the order that he has given to me. When received, these objects confirm the strength of corresponding houses in the Chart that we just made based on Aaroodh etc.

In my opinion, Telegnosis is all about answering a question and hence, the Houses are more important than the Chart showing all planets. Further, we need not stop here; as this are just some of the many methods we are going to use.

Now, see some details of the directions, Sheershoday, etc., specific to Raashi :-

SN	Raashi	Direction	Tattv	Movement	Limb ruled	Uday/Rise	Colour
1	Mesh	East	Fire	Mobile	Head	Prush-today	Red
2	Vrushabh	East	Earth	Steady	Face	Prush-today	White
3	Mithun	Agni	Vaayu	Mixed	Chest	Sheer-shoday	Green
4	Kark	South	Water	Mobile	Heart	Prush-today	Pink
5	Simh	South	Fire	Steady	Stom-ach	Sheer-shoday	Yellow
6	Kanyaa	Nairutya	Earth	Mixed	Waist	Sheer-shoday	Mixed
7	Tulaa	West	Vaayu	Mobile	Abdo-men	Sheer-shoday	Dark
8	Vrush-chik	West	Water	Steady	Geni-tals	Sheer-shoday	Gold-en

9	Dhanu	Vaayavya	Fire	Mixed	Thighs	Prush-today	Yellow
10	Makar	North	Earth	Mobile	Knees	Prush-today	Mixed
11	Kumbh	North	Vaayu	Steady	Lower legs	Sheer-shoday	Brown
12	Meen	Ishaanya	Water	Mixed	Feet	Ubha-yoday	Blue

Prushtoday Signs when rise on horizon, the back side rises first, unlike the rise of Sheershoday (where the head comes first); and in Ubhayoday the head and back both rise together. Meen is the only Raashi that is Ubhayoday Raashi. About questions, the Sheershoday Lagn or Aaroodh show favourable situations.

Note on visualizing the Prashn Purush or Bhaav Purush

In the example above, we have Vrushabh Ascendant : Sun is in 9th House ruled by Makar, and Moon is in (say) 8th House ruled by Jupiter. Vrushabh, as the Ascendant is a slow moving Raashi, indicating shoulders and family as per tables given elsewhere in this book. The 9th House indicates dutifulness and long travels etc. and Moon is in 8th House (dealing with longevity in this case), which is ruled by Jupiter in this case. Ascendant is a beneficial, 9th House is a good House and Sun is expected to add power to that; and Moon, though placed in 8th House, the House of death etc., is ruled by Jupiter, in this case. The overall primary observation is indicative of a good possibility of success. As we grow, we get more experience of taking a holistic view of such situations where all planets are placed in the horoscope; and a comparative study is taken on hand. Such exercises are generally lengthy and can be done when astrologer is given enough time. Good if it is possible, but for Telegnosis, the above is enough, and is in no way less than required.

Let us keep in mind at this juncture that when we have Vrushabh Lagn (whether by traditional or Aaroodh calculations), we need to make a rough picture in mind that the question or querist's body starts with (Vrushabh) Taurus. In other words, his head and nature will be like a Vrushabh-ruled person has, and going in that way, his feet will fall in Mesh (or Aries). This is the art of visualizing the Bhaav Purush or Prashn Purush. One should also know that in this case, Shukra being the Lord of Vrushabh also influences Head, and in that order, Mangal, the Lord of Mesh, the twelfth House, affects the feet: Maybe the person has problems of injury or perspiration or bleeding in and around his feet. It is seen that generally people keep on touching their body parts, very often indicative of that being the seat of trouble.

Once the Lagn, the Raashi or the Constellation, rising on East horizon is known, the chart becomes easy. Astrologer can place the position of major planets as shown in the Almanac or based on information published in daily newspapers. Now, predictions can be made, based on the inter se impact of planets. At this stage, we stop to remind our readers that though predictions can be and are being made, based on such charts, it is advisable to crosscheck the predictions considering the other methods of foretelling, that, together, make Telegnosis. We will also discuss a few more methods in separate chapters.

Some special observations
In a horoscope, the 5th House indicates mainly the children, education, short journeys etc., and the following will add to

the astrological judgement. In our opinion, the information as given below, if shared with querist, will increase respect for astrologer:-

If this star is present in Aaroodh or 5th House	Result (for querist before this meeting)
Rahu/ Shani	The querist may have met bad people on way
Mangal	The querist may have met quarrelsome people
Budh	The querist may have met low people like servants
Guru	The querist may have met literate Guru
Shukra	The querist may have met clean and bright people
Sun	The querist may have met or seen administrators
Moon	The querist may have met decent females

The Eighth House deals with different types of losses, and we can see the result of different stars occupying that position from Aaroodh or Lagn in a Kundali. This information can be of use in course of answering the questions and to scale up respect for astrology in general:-

If 8th from Aaroodh or Lagn is	Result (for querist before this meeting)
Sun	Royal displeasure, more so on previous Sunday
Moon	Hunger, thirst, more so on previous Monday

Mangal	Fall, injury, more so on previous Tuesday
Budh	Loss due to quarrel on previous Wednesday
Guru	Religious mistakes more so on previous Thursday
Shukra	Family dispute more so on previous Friday
Shani	Overall loss more so on previous Saturday
Rahu	Injury on Right foot on upper side
Ketu	Injury on Left foot on lower side

Notes

Basic Astrology - Bhaav and Planets

In a birth chart or a Horary Chart, the first House is considered as Lagn, where we place the Raashi, rising on the East horizon at that time. After that, planets are placed as per the current positions.

The main planets, considered by Indian astrologers are nine, viz., Sun, Moon, Mangal, Budh, Guru, Shukra, Shani, Rahu and Ketu. The last two are the reference points cutting the Solar orbit into two equal halves at that time. Let us summarily see special features assigned to these planets which are characterised as if in a film!

We give a Table, which is illustrative in nature, and is not exhaustive.

Sr. No.	Planet	Indicative subjects/ Inferential conclusions etc.
1	Sun	Father, administrative authority, boldness, honey eyes, upper abdomen, Fiery element, fearless, masculine. It also represents fatherly personality; wavering lights, bones in the body.

2	Moon	Mother, affectionate, walks with limp, white, cool, chest, God fearing, dependent, feminine, likes water, beautiful, fast moving. It also represents rainy season, motherly affections, watery eyes; and blood in the body.
3	Mangal	Brother, bold, warrior, physically energetic, violent, shoulders, red eyes, mark of injury on face, masculine, likes competition, youth, cruelty, landed property, courage, summer; muscles in the body.
4	Budh	Teacher, Thinker, talker, philosopher, yellow colour/ eyes, not bold, physically weak, gaseous, Neurological systems, neutral gender. It also represents knowledge, mental health, green colour, speech, Sharad Ritu; and skin quality in human body.
5	Guru	Professor, Prime Minister, Preacher, tall, hefty structure, impressive, leader, masculine. It also represents experience-based knowledge, intellect, wisdom, bodily health, and honey colour.

6	Shukra	Preacher, feminine, tall, slim structure, leader, attractive, shining skin, likes perfumes, genitals. It also represents happiness from vehicles, spouse, sex, and is indicated by mixed colours.
7	Shani	Small eyes, observant, skilful, politician, cunning, slow moving, dirty, gaseous. It also represents death, causes of death, imprisonment, sorrows, chronic diseases; and neurological system in human body.
8	Rahu	Cunning/ liar, suicidal or killer instincts, upper foot, like Shani. It also represents extreme disorders relating skin, eye and legs.
9	Ketu	Almost like Mangal, rules lower feet.

Bhaav

A Birth Chart always has 12 houses. They are numbered anticlockwise or from Left to Right side. The planets are placed in respective House according to their current position in the Sky at that point of time. The daily planetary positions are available in Almanac. These positions are also generally printed in all major daily newspapers almost in all countries.

In Telegnosis, there are techniques where the entire Horoscope together with these Houses is 'seen' as a human body, a bungalow, a garden etc., divided equally in twelve parts. Each House traditionally denotes varying interpretation depending upon its being occupied by a planet and inter se distance from each other. It is not possible to explain entire Horoscopy in a single small chapter like this. It is the exclusive and individual art of interpretation, based on position of these planets within these twelve Houses. Bhrigu Samhitaa, Brihat Samhitaa etc., are the major compilations of the principles of making predictions, and also a huge number of horoscopes; and therefor a study of these Samhitaa will make one wiser to foretell more correctly. For Telegnosis, we are more concerned with placement of the Sun and the Moon; and the Ascendant (the first House); and with what these twelve houses stand for in general. Let us firm up these factors in our mind and take advantage of these methods of foretelling. The following Table is illustrative in nature, and is not exhaustive:-

Sr. No.	House	Indicative subjects/ Inferential conclusions etc.
1	1st	Self, Head, face. It also represents health, gait (typical style of walking), fame, shape of body, habits.
2	2nd	It represents one's own family and family wealth, right eye, General Knowledge, quality of voice etc.
3	3rd	Younger brother and sisters, Helpers like army at command, Eye (Right), ability to take actions. It also represents right ear, internal courage. Mental work. Planning, and execution.
4	4th	Mother, Protection, Happiness from within, Chest in human body, style of sitting/ posture, sleeping place and bed, Water storages, landed property, treasury.

5	5th	Children, short travels, Art, Upper stomach, Education, intellect, memory, memory of past birth, advising ability, ability to arrive at correct judgement/ conclusions, oratory, black magic; an ambassador.
6	6th	Job, competition, enemies, lower stomach, maternal uncles, breaks in profession, mental illness, death due to accident or injury etc, fear from servants and thieves.
7	7th	Life partner, sex partners, and business partners. Partnerships in general. Genitals. It also represents Social relations, style of sleeping, Effective communication skill or otherwise, water in rivers, secret wealth.
8	8th	Death, fatal accidents, longevity, anus and buttocks in human body. It also represents disasters, dangers, defamation, place and cause of natural death, long duration illnesses, fear of enemies; and lost assets.
9	9th	Dutifulness, honesty, long travels, Upper legs, presence of fatherly figures around, willingness to donate, role as spiritual guide, grandchildren, stored water, temples and spirituality.
10	10th	Father, Goal of life, level of success, Lower legs. It also represents temples, type of assistance received, service in Court or Administration, Style or standing posture; amount of rain in state. Historical transactions.
11	11th	Gains from life (business), elder brothers and sisters, Upper foot. It also represents left ear/ hand and income generation.

12	12th	Loss, Cause of death, punishments, previous birth, Suicide, Lower feet, donations and charity, left eye, break in career, sinful acts, physical disabilities etc. Vairaagya in mind.

It is added that seers can deduce many things about the messenger (sent by querist) from the 11th House; and surprisingly, many features become evident about the Astrologer himself based on 12th House as said in Prashn Marg. It is expected that the students of astrology conduct a good number of experiments to verify these Sootra.

In Telegnosis, interpretation of Bhaav (each House) is of the highest importance. Suppose, we want to examine the Kundali of a person's spouse, the Seventh House could be treated as 1st House. That will 'serve' the purpose of the Birth Chart of his wife. In the same way, if we want to know about the father in law of the querist, we can take 4th House as Lagn because it is 10th from the 7th House! In other words, it is the House of father of wife of the querist. Taking this art of interpretation to a next higher level, we can examine relation of querist with his children by examining his 5th house, but the relation of the same children with his wife is to be seen from 11th House in his Kundali which is 5th from 7th House! Thus, astrological prediction is largely an art of endless interpretations of Bhaav and Planets placed therein like this.

Table showing Raashi. An illustrative table is given below which is not exhaustive (please read as if a person is standing face to face before the astrologer) :-

SN	Raashi	Indicative subjects/ Inferential conclusions etc.
1	Mesh	Head, Ruled by Mars, Mobile/ quick, East, Female, Fire. It also represents gold mines, canals, places where serpents stay, forest, afraid of water (Nature: Kshatriya, hot tempered)
2	Vrushabh	Shoulders, ruled by Venus, Slow moving, East, Male, Earth. It also represents cultivable soil, income generating assets like FDs, Cows, beautiful locations to stay. Ability to tackle big responsibilities, good colleague, strong. (Nature: Bargaining Vaishya)
3	Mithun	Intellect, Ruled by Mercury, Mixed nature, Agni (South East), Vayu. It also represents gardens, temples, palaces, and townships, likes music etc, tall, orator. (Nature: Skilled labour and architect)
4	Kark	Chest, Ruled by Moon, quick Mobile, South, Female, Water. It also represents neighbourhood, respectful relations with opposite sex, places of worship, watery places, multifaceted, good student, dutiful, fond of travel. (Nature: Pious brahmin)

5	Simh	Upper stomach, Ruled by Sun, Slow moving, South, Male, Fire. It also represents forests, mountains, and high society culture, likes cool climate, bold, royal in nature, strong, healthy. (Nature: Kshatriya)
6	Kanyaa	Lower stomach, Ruled by Mercury, Mixed nature, Nairutya, Earth. It also represents sea coast, ladies' hostels, small vehicles, temples, poet, popular, art-lover, meticulous. (Nature: Expert trader, Vaishya)
7	Tulaa	Genitals, Ruled by Venus, Quick moving, West, Female, Vayu. It also represents market places, small greeneries around towns etc; smart, popular among friends. (Nature: Skilled in bargaining, inferior to Vaishya).
8	Vrushchik	Anus, Ruled by Mars, Slow moving, West, Male, likes water, ruthless, cruel, researcher. It also represents stored water (ponds, wells etc.) (Nature: Preacher, Brahmin)
9	Dhanu	Upper legs, ruled by Jupiter, Mixed nature, Vaayavya (N West), Fire. It also represents guesthouses, battlefield, constructions of all types of artificial waterbodies like dams, and forest land, fearless, scientist, orator, sculptor, fat in body, frank in discussion. (Nature: Kshatriya)

10	Makar	Lower legs, Ruled by Saturn, Quick, North, Female, Earth. It also represents rivers rivulets, places where tribes stay, cities on river banks, Lazy, yellowish, honest, music lover, large family, attractive, thinker. (Nature: Vaishya)
11	Kumbh	Upper feet, ruled by Saturn, Slow moving, North, Male, Vayu. It also represents stored waterbodies. It also shows secrecy in all matters, does charity, affectionate, self-made. (Nature: Skilled in secrets, like police and spy)
12	Meen	Lower feet, ruled by Jupiter, Mixed nature, Ishaan (North East), Water. It also represents expertise in arts, fast decisions, popular persons, lack of confidence water creeks, big temples, and violent rivers. (Nature: Brahmin)

Some more observations need to be kept in view that Moon, Mercury, Venus and Jupiter are considered as good and friendly Planets, but Sun, Mars, Saturn, Rahu and Ketu are considered not so good. In a nutshell, we can say that good planets are good everywhere, but the bad planets are good only if they are in bad Houses like 6, 8, and 12. The good or bad is also to be seen with reference to Planet's distance from Lagn and from its own Rashi. Here, we will briefly understand the meaning of the word distance. Every planet aspects (fully) the House opposite to its placement which is 7th from its position. Jupiter aspects also 5th and 9th House from where it is posited, Shani aspects 3rd and 10th House in addition to the 7th House; and Mangal aspects 4th and 8th House fully in addition to 7th House. In support of this it is said that the 'Seeing' or 'Aspecting' is ¾ of the full impact, on 4th and 8th Houses from where it is posited; ½ of the full impact on 5th and 9th Houses; and ¼ of its impact on the 3rd and 10th Houses where a planet is posited. Such an aspecting decides the strength or a mood of the Planets in a Horoscope. By this, we mean that these planets can substantially influence those Houses and also the planets 'seated' in those Houses. Suppose, Shani, seated in first House, aspects Sun, posited in 10th, it will spoil results of that House which generally indicates father, and main profession of the querist. When a similar chart is made with reference to presentment of a specific question, the art of foretelling is called Horary Astrology. It is as if a person/ question is born at that time. The experts prefer to compare a Natal chart (balance of past Karm) with the Horary chart (result of actions taken recently) and see whether the both the charts are in conformity. If there is a good degree of correlation, it basically means that the present situation is in conformity with the previous deeds, and that the question will be easy to realize, and vice versa.

As already said in some chapters, the Rishi, based on centuries of observations, have skilfully assigned each routine to specific planets, specific Raashi and Nakshatra. Thus, there exists a lot of symbolism in predictive astrology. It, therefore, is necessary that in place of mugging up the illustrations given in various Samhitaa, it is helpful to understand the underlying principles.

Raashi, Planets & their transit

As said elsewhere, sages have distributed every visible and invisible thing in this universe among the 12 Rashi, 12 Bhaav and have also described impact of each planet travelling or posited in these celestial places. There is such huge literature complied by sages that one can keep reading for the entire life, and still much will be left unread. In view of this, we present below some indicative tables which will be of good help with regard to answering routine questions presented before astrologers:-

Impact of Planets in 12 House/ Bhaav while **dealing with questions**
SUN

Bhaav	Prominent feature of Sun if posited/ passing through these Bhaav
1	May cause loss of movable property
2	Loss of currency, money, value
3	Possibility of gains from elders
4	Loss of respect, reputation
5	Mental worries of short term
6	Victory over competitors
7	Loss in monetary terms
8	Bodily pains and injuries

9	Loss of enthusiasm and working capability
10	Achievement or accomplishment of task on hand
11	Gains in some tangible form
12	Loss in tangible form

MOON

Bhaav	Prominent feature of Moon if posited/ passing through these Bhaav
1	Satisfaction of sorts
2	Loss of familial property
3	Success with help of relatives (like younger brothers)
4	Get motherly affection, some worries reducing happiness
5	Mental worries
6	Profit due to defeat of competitors
7	Friendship or intimacy with spouse
8	Unnecessary expenses causing worries
9	Administrative problems, Raids on business places etc.
10	Absolute satisfaction – maybe due to appreciation from family/ king
11	Gains – maybe with help of elder brothers etc.
12	General losses

MANGAL/ Mars

Bhaav	Prominent feature of Mangal if posited/ passing through these Bhaav
1	Competitors may take over
2	Loss of landed property owned by family

3	Gains due to efforts of younger brothers and sisters
4	Business competition with less hope to tackle
5	Short term loss in studies/ investments etc.
6	Short term gains due to victory over colleagues
7	Some small disease related with the limb indicated by that Rashi
8	Competitors may become powerful
9	Bodily pains as per limb ruled by Rashi of the House
10	Uneasiness due to circumstances – maybe legal framework
11	All types of gains
12	Physical diseases, accidents, injuries

BUDH/ Mercury

Bhaav	Prominent feature of Guru if posited/ passing through these Bhaav
1	Some danger of accident on head or the limb indicated by Rashi
2	Gain due to family efforts
3	Some displacement or movement/ change in place/ policy
4	Social gains/ reputation/ family gatherings
5	General happiness
6	Increase in enmity/ disease
7	Increase in reputation – maybe due to partners
8	Health Issues causing expenses
9	Increase in profit/ Royal honours

10	Loss of reputation/ Raids/ punishments/ Demotion
11	Big gains, Royal honours, felicitations
12	Diseases related to the limb, indicated by the Rashi

GURU/ Jupiter

Bhaav	Prominent feature of Guru if posited/ passing through these Bhaav
1	Some danger of accident on head or the limb indicated by Rashi
2	Gain due to family efforts
3	Some displacement or movement/ change in place/ policy
4	Social gains/ reputation/ family gatherings
5	General happiness
6	Increase in enmity/ disease
7	Increase in reputation – maybe due to partners
8	Health Issues causing expenses
9	Increase in profit/ Royal honours
10	Loss of reputation/ Raids/ punishments/ Demotion
11	Big gains, Royal honours, felicitations
12	Diseases related to the limb, indicated by the Rashi

Shukra/ Venus

Bhaav	Prominent feature of Shukra if posited/ passing through these Bhaav
1	Desired pleasure

2	Family may help in gaining property
3	Younger brothers etc may cause gains
4	Expected happiness may become realise
5	Birth in family/ Short term friendships
6	Competitors may become powerful, conspiracy etc.
7	May affect internal happiness due to arguments etc.
8	Monetary savings/ gains/ Insurance etc., related with health issues
9	Legitimate profits in business on a big scale
10	May cause loss of internal happiness
11	Monetary profits – maybe with help of elders
12	Expenses relating to investment opportunities, that may cause loss

SHANI/ Saturn

Bhaav	Prominent feature of Shani if posited/ passing through these Bhaav
1	Physical disease (as per Rashi in that House)
2	Loss mostly in Family property
3	Profits due to hard work of assistants
4	General unhappiness
5	Short term loss
6	Short term profits caused due to problems faced by enemies
7	Sudden travel/ change of place of business or even residence
8	Body pain caused as per the limb indicated by Rashi of the Bhaav

9	Unhappiness (maybe due to spiritual matters/ confusions)
10	Physical and social weakness – maybe due to powerful opponents
11	Attaining satisfaction after hard-work of years
12	Loss of reputation mostly due to wrongful infor-mation

As regards Rahu and Ketu, the result could be comparable with Shani and Mangal as indicated above.

Notes

LakshaN

Telegnosis heavily depends upon LakshaN – the art of interpretation of LakshaNs, happening around while the question is being answered. It presupposes art of drawing inference based on the subtle changes so occurring in the environment at that time. LakshaN could be defined as the sign or a symptom, seen, experienced, noted, learnt, understood by the astrologer which foretells certain result in connection with a specific situation presented before him for a possible solution. It is called omen in English. It is important to note that in famous work Prashn Marg, LakshaN and Shakun seem to be included in the term Nimitt. The readers are requested to draw appropriate meaning of these terms, which are generally used as Tatkaal LakshaN or spontaneous omens.

It is generally external and becomes part of inferential knowledge like a smoke indicates possibility of a fire in that direction or at that place. It can be said that LakshaN is the language that the Mother Nature speaks. The important question comes, now. Who teaches and guides the animals! How do they decide? Is it that for them, the direct and the indirect evidence (the Pratyaksh and the Anumaan) are interwoven! Let us stop for a second and think. When the animals and birds see the black clouds, they come to know (if not much before that) the direction and possible velocity and humidity in the blowing wind, and they are also able to field any other sounds present around them at that time; and they try to take appropriate action to save their younger ones! The question also comes how certain birds fly over the oceans that too for months that too in a direction (without a compass) for thousands of kilometres for breeding! How the entire flock reaches at desired place and land every year! How do ants locate sugar in a big hall and line up to consume it! How does the meat fly come to know that there is a dead body around! How do the birds like crow make nests at a certain height and in a direction, which is safe for breeding much before the actual rains! How do the animals escape place of earthquake or tsunami much before it strikes! There must be something that we, humans, have missed so far.

These animals and birds do not have any ways to compile and pass on the wisdom to the next generation but are able to save their life and that their 'societies' are as they were before centuries! They must be having their own doctors and police and such other departments to administer good normal life; and that they do not have wars like we have. They do not kill fellow beings for survival the way we do. I think they understand the Nature more than us. Perhaps, LakshaN Shaastra has gone deep into their DNA. Such things tell us that there exists such a language that these animals trust and take due advantage of the same. Why, we humans have carefully decided to be the last beneficiary of these LakshaN? On the contrary, we prefer to laugh at this! Let us make a beginning to take advantage.

In Telegnosis, importance is given to internal as well as external indications. We need to hear what the Nature wants to communicate at a given point of time. It is believed that nothing happens without a reason. Everything communicates, provided we have art of perceiving it and interpreting it. We need to take a photograph of Nature, let it be called an Environmentograph. This term speaks for itself. These are all time-tested inferences and need to be kept in view at all points of time.

LakshaN also speak for internal state of mind. LakshaN can be seen in the Nature, humans and animals with a trained eye. In Communication, it is said that "you cannot not communicate". In crude sense, it is called body language or Kinesics. LakshaN shaastra is a very old compilation of observations in ancient Indian books, but good that it is being studied by many behavioural scientists and curators of many animal zoo units in West. Such studies would add to the collective wisdom to save a lot of avoidable inconvenience in future if taught to this generation anew. We see that even the most fashionable actresses bite their nails before the Miss World Awards are announced; we also see highly educated scientists shaking their foot while thinking; we see many politicians crossing their legs and arms while attending a meeting; and we see the wisest judge perspiring while talking to ministers. We see that the doctors who are cancer patients are no less afraid of death than the normal non-medico patients! The body does speak, and others can 'hear'.

When we read the ancient books there, we find examples of some learned persons who knew 'language' of birds, animals and even trees! Is it not a science of interpreting the environment which is apparently dead! Sages were able to answer genuine questions without use of Almanac. They, remaining seated at one place for days, were able to answer a series of questions based on the same environment, because the same set up had differing connotations about different questions. In Sanskrit, it is said that 'Sansarati Iti Sansaarah' and 'Jam Gachchati Iti Jagat' (Sansaar is what is constantly moving, Jagat is what is constantly travelling to some place). In view of this ever-changing environment, there cannot be one answer to two questions and otherwise. The Sages were able to see the minute changes, taking place every second. Maybe they mastered Traatak and Naad at a very primary level of their training or schooling under Indian Knowledge Systems (IKS).

RaamaayaN and Mahaabhaarat, the two are not only major sources, replete with knowledge and Bhaaratiya lifestyle, but are also indicative of many other branches of knowledge known as LakshaN, Nimitt, Shagun, medicine, Upavaas, Yaatu (magical results of sound frequencies etc. as indicated in Atharv Ved) etc. These also have many references to Astrology, for example they give us celestial positions at the time of birth of Bhagavaan Raam and KrishN, and also at the time of the great war with RaavaN and at the time of War in Kurukshetra. Dr. Nilesh Oak has mathematically and very logically proved this based on most advanced software, available in the West in his presentations on YouTube. It is to be noted that Valmeeki, wrote RaamaayaN much before the birth of Bhagaavan Raam! Even veterans like Svami Dayanand Sarasvati who outrightly rejected use of Astrology, as being used to read horoscope of individuals, would find it difficult to challenge the foresight of Valmeeki in this case! What I want to say is that, it is difficult to reject anything available in an intelligent human mind which is capable of reading, understanding, interpreting, and using the knowledge emanating from Universe: The universe does have a language, and it does speak. If it is not audible or visible or available to me, it is not that it does not exist anywhere. Suppose I do not have a television set in my house that does not mean that those waves are not there, yes, I am not equipped to receive the same. Like that, We have to believe that the Universe does communicate with all of us at all times and at all places, and that we can realize the same if we are trained to receive the signals like those who have divine soul like Valmeeki, and that if we accept that we are also gifted like those animals who flee the places before tsunami or earthquake; and of course, and if we are prepared to train or tune our brain faculties by methods like Traatak, suggested by the Sages.

LakshaN and general observations

In the above background, we can straight away come to the subject. Whenever a person puts a genuine question for seeking its answer, the answer is not only hidden in his own words, but it is very much reflected in his actions and gestures. The trained eye of the astrologer does not miss those actions because half of the answer is present there, the other half is present in form of various LakshaN in the environment. Following are some of the very general actions made by the querist; the respective interpretations are given by the side of each one. I am sure that for new entrants, the following table will amount to a good beginning of a long journey of Astrology which was taught in Gurukul for about 12 years from very young age:-

SN	LakshaN	Prediction
1	The question is put with confusion and thoughtfulness	Bad.
2	The question is put with breaks	Breaks
3	If someone walks between querist and astrologer	Interruption

4	If querist beats himself like for killing mosquito etc.	Defeat
5	If querist yawns	Bad
6	If querist breaks some articles kept near him for any reason	Bad
7	If querist uproots grass, tears some paper etc.	Bad
8	If he tightens his necktie or binds himself with some rope etc.	Bad
9	If he has worn dirty clothes, if he smears himself with dirt/ ash etc.	Bad
10	If wears flower or garments of red or white flowers	Bad
11	If repeatedly looks at some bad objects/ picture	Bad
12	If he praises pictures of war, dead persons, or such posters	Bad
13	If he touches circular objects	Unending matter
14	If he pokes fingers in some holes anywhere/ body (nose etc.)	Bad character
15	If a good pandit or friend/ bad person/ stranger arrives	Good/ Bad
16	If a lamp gets extinguished without any reason	Bad
17	If good music or a prayer is heard at the time of discussion	Good
18	If unacceptable noise/ dialogue is heard during discussion	Bad

19	If a nice young girl arrives/an elephant/ an ox is seen/ heard	Good
20	In case of theft, if question is uttered in breaks	Bad
21	Good/ domestic animals are seen in odd number 1,3,5,7	Good
22	Seeing of brahmin/ liquor, fresh food, jewel, new clothes, fragrant flowers	Good
23	Seeing utensils, furniture, vehicles are seen upside down	Bad
24	Seeing good articles, pleasing pictures like waterfall	Good
25	If he touches his toe on any feet	Illness (self)
26	If he touches any of his toes of his feet	Illness of ward
27	If querist draws some good articles, and picks up any	Good
28	If head or other limb of querist get hurt at that time	Bad for king

About some Shapes and directions of objects

Whenever we see (even in dreams) any things, each has certain meaning. Some important features are given below which may come handy in Telegnosis:-

1. An upward triangle indicates a masculine gender and fire element, and

2. A downward triangle indicates feminine gender and watery element;

3. Any object that is horizontal, more so if it is not generally found in that way, indicates neutral gender: A tree is generally expected to be seen upward, or a rocket is

expected to be built upward, but if such objects are seen or heard to be in horizontal position, it is indicative of neutral gender;

4. A circular motion indicates Vayu tattv: better if clockwise. If an object has four sides, like in a square or rectangle, it stands for Earthly element;

5. but if it has more than four angles and side and is irregular in shape, it indicates Aakash Tattv; and

6. If we see a dot or a point or a Bindu, stands either for a new beginning or the end of the objective of the question.

Raja Nal and Language of animals

Many PuraaN have reference to this system of predictions in day to day life. As a sequel to this, it is better to note that Kipling has created an imaginary character of Mowgli who understands and communicates with all animals in forest, and that in India this has been well understood and is recorded as much systematically as stories of King Nal and King Yudhishthir who could communicate with trees and plants! In the books on Ayurved, it is written that medicinal plants in and around crematoria should be avoided for patients. In RaamaayaN, we find the famous dialogue between Mother Seeta and Jataayu - who was a bird! In India, thus, we have already recognized capacity of trees to tell something to us and capacity of humans to understand the same! I feel that the receiver, the human in our discussion today, should train himself to learn to be more alert, and be wiser based on everything around us. Omens are to be seen with regard to areas (for example the rural and urban animals); heavenly reference (sky watching); relating to day or night hours; some are season-specific; some are related to flying birds and some relate to the animal that swim; and some are related to insects and snacks etc.

While Ayurved says Sachetanaah Vrukshaah (Trees are alive), Jagadeesh Chandra Basu proved in previous century by machines that they do show emotions! Telegnosis does consider these subtle signals for answering a genuine question.

In Europe, I understand that they predict the forthcoming year being good or bad depending upon who comes first on the night on 31 December every year. I think it is termed as "First Foot". There may be many such illustrations which need to be studied anew. On the face of it, such things can be straight away brushed aside as being unscientific because it requires efforts to falsify it or verify it! I feel that preconditioned or biased minds cannot explore new areas or the areas that need more experiments and database.

A Jain Aagam book was published in Gujarati where ample illustrations were given as to how kings used to take notes of animal behaviour and animal language (sound). Behaviour refers to their clockwise or anti clockwise movements, jumping, dancing, mating, flying downward or upward or in a direction either in a group or otherwise etc.; and the animal sounds refer to cooing and barking vehemently or otherwise. Ayurved (Charak) says that Parrot, Cow, Crow, Peacock, Horse, Dog and a few more, more so the female species, have inherent ability to sense potential danger, presence of deadly poison in food articles (if presented before them), and express by their sounds, their language. Each species reacts in different way showing specific LakshaN as observed by Sages. I have seen crows avoiding fresh blood of chicken mixed with simple rice, offered after rites on seashore of Mumbai! In this case, they all flew away from their otherwise favourite food, being expected to be consumed by them! But none of the crows touched it, rather all flew far away from that small group as if they were afraid of something. I also recall that in thick forest of Junagadh, when the cows take a U turn to return to temple, at that very moment, the young calves start jumping though their respective mothers are miles away. When the goats return home, their respective younger ones identify their mothers from the entire herd. All this is indicative of the accurate memory and sensing ability of animals and birds; and we need to take note of all these for appropriate use of these features while making predictions under Telegnosis.

We all know that particularly when killer earthquake struck on the western coast of India on 26th January 2001, no animals had died of the earthquake. All free animals had fled the places and were living in open areas. I have seen fishes trying to jump from the water of the small ponds in Digha, a coastal town in West Bengal; I could predict that some natural calamity was to take place. On the next morning, Police was announcing on loudspeakers that no one should visit the coast as tsunami was expected. Before the machines could sense the epi-centre, these illiterate fishes had come to know that tsunami was directed to their town! Brihat Samhitaa has many chapters on Omens relating to birds and beasts. In a nutshell, it can be concluded that the animals considered and called as a male in general are good if seen on the left side; while the animals considered as females, are good if seen on the right hand side while proceeding on a mission.

Smell and Voice – as a tool for diagnosis
Recently, a Health Voice Centre under Florida University conducted an experiment by medical doctors to use voice samples of thousands of people to make a diagnosis of their disease, and they published some results that from the audio

frequencies of these people, fluency and their tone etc., they were able to know that what was the disease. Certain commonalities were observed in the voice, irrespective of age and gender, among the patients having same disease! News about this experiment was published in a reputed Gujarati daily Divyabhaskar in its edition dated 12 October 2022. This exactly is what has been used in ancient Indian Knowledge System, which is the basis of Telegnosis. It is said that a feminine voice produces 250 cycles per second as against 150 produced by voice of a male. The voice hearing machine seems to be capable of processing such finer aspects.

If we go deep into this, we see that every animal has been gifted with some unique system for ensuring better and safe survival. Ants sense the immediate rains, dogs have capacity to memorize smell for even three months. It is said that human nose has 50 lakh cells while dog's nose has 2200 lakh cells which makes it possible to identify the smell, which is used by Police and Bomb diffusing squads very regularly. Recently, a famous military dog named Zoom died in Kashmir in Aug 2022 who was given a proper funeral with respect. It is reported that some months before in the year 2021, US marines used dogs to kill Baghdadi, the notorious leader of an international terrorist organization. Even Courts of Law are willing to admit evidences fielded by such dogs in certain cases. Gujarati daily Divyabhaskar, in its edition dated 17 January 2023, reported that as a part of strengthening security prior to parade on 26 January, Police have started special training to 26 dogs that can detect/ smell drugs even less than 1 gram; and even explosives also! It is said that from age of 3-5 months, these puppies are given 6 month training for such expertise. It is also reported that a dog, named Java, traced the rapist in Karajan successfully. Slowly, we are in process of recognizing the special abilities like these for doing justice and thereby making the life a just affair. She-pigeons are being used for aerial communication between kingdoms, cities and lovers from time immemorial.

Similarly, experiments have been reported to have been conducted by team of doctors where smell of the body of patients is used for diagnosis. Perhaps, they are using trained dogs to smell and communicate to the trainers as to their findings. In India, we do believe that certain animals show this capacity by making some special sound or movement and foretell the disease or an event or a strong possibility. That is what we mean by LakshaN.

Considering the above information, we, now, will see a few prominent illustrations which may relate to a variety of fields. Reader may extend the experience gained from such illustrations to the real-life situations. The intention is to highlight applicability of Telegnosis in all walks of life. About Telegnosis, if these LakshaN are taken into consideration, a lot of expenditure on unnecessary Pathological and Radiological tests can be saved. At least till the time these laboratories reduce their fees to an acceptable and affordable level, Telegnosis could be taken up as an experiment.

Brihat Samhitaa, the most read book among astrologers in India, has many chapters of LakshaN. We find a useful analysis of external and internal LakshaN. An understanding arises that while LakshaN could be internal (as Risht) as well external (Cloud formation), the Shakun (and Nimitta) could be generally external. The Samhitaa contains full-fledged chapters on movements, behaviour and sound of animals like cows, jackals, dogs. It deals with cawing of crows in good details that, if fly during night hours, foretell a natural calamity in that area. It also says that what a crow brings in (his beak) is gained and what it takes, goes away! If they caw at Sun in Ishaanya, East or Agni, being seated on a wall, the owner suffers in terms of health and wealth. Let us see some of the interesting observations with reference to a dog:

Dogs:
If two dogs bark at the rising Sun, one can expect change in Administration (Mayor, Collector, Minister);
If dogs bark in this way during noon hours, some big fire and loot is expected, more so if they face South-West;
If such barking is seen in evening hours, some problems is expected in agricultural operations;
If during night, dogs go inside temple or stand on hay or grass and start barking, this indicates death of important person in the area; if this happens during monsoon, it indicates heavy rain in a day or two;
If during famine days, dogs jump into water and dance, good rains are expected after 12 days;
If a dog keeps his body outside the door, and cries with his mouth inside, more so looking at the landlady, some serious sickness could be expected in a week;
The things that a dog scratches inside the house/ campus, get badly affected; and
If a dog produces sneezing like sound and encircles a person, he should drop journey.

Ayurved has rich chapters on Risht LakshaN. It is said that the patients invariably show typical LakshaN before death, and these LakshaN differ in each major disease, listed there in those chapters. It is advised in the books of Ayurved that on seeing these Risht LakshaN, the patient should be treated with utmost kindness and the relatives should be tactfully informed. Such an information adds to the reputation of treating doctor and Ayurved, both; on the contrary, if still doctor continues the treatment, over a period of time, people lose faith in such doctors and ultimately in the Ayurved also.

Each person, being an independent individual, does have his own LakshaN. Animals also communicate and receive these messages. No two persons or animals are a perfect copy. Hence it is important to train our eyes to note the uniqueness of a person or an object before us. Based on those typical LakshaN, it may be possible to identify the uniqueness. Today, the machines are put to this work where they identify people based on their iris, fingerprint, DNA etc., tomorrow, it will be possible to identify people based on body smell etc., But, the animals are already doing it! We have already seen examples of a few animals and birds. Telegnosis tries to take advantage of those instincts and LakshaN. LakshaN Shaastra alone can explain many questions like the following ones:-

1. Why animals bite or attack certain persons only? I know some people in this category.
2. Why calves of a certain cow only get killed by wild animals ? The shepherds experience such things.
3. Why some women face abortion tragedy every time? A professor of Gynaecology has this problem which was unanswered for his entire youth!

We are going to note a few observations made by our seniors which we are tempted to undermine because the same are not respectfully discussed in today's day to day life. But that does not render them irrelevant anymore, the animal kingdom still follows the natural language and takes advantage to save their life. The subject happens to be as big as this universe and therefore, any write up cannot be made more indicative than being done here.

LakshaNs and diseases

In the ancient times, there was a tradition of inviting the doctor for a visit. It is said that each omen on the way is important and is indicative of future of the patient. It is said that no patient dies without the Risht LakshaN. Risht are general as well as specific to each disease. Let us quickly see what Sushrut and Vaagbhat have said on such Risht LakshaN.:-

SN	Risht - LakshaN (attention is attracted generally to the bad indications because there is no need to point out if treatment is working fine)	Whether Good or Bad
1	When a wound does not heal and gives bad smell, is cold on borders	Bad/ death
2	When a wound is surrounded by some dusty material	Bad
3	When a wound does not heal despite a Mantra (Shaabar mantra work)	Bad
4	When the messenger comes from south or faces south	Bad
5	When the messenger tumbles or hit on way	Bad
6	When messenger & patient belong to different classes or castes	Bad
7	When the messenger if afraid, and falters while speaking	Bad
8	When messenger is dirty - with smeared clothes & shoes	Bad
9	When the messenger is riding a black or dirty vehicle	Bad
10	When messenger of a Kaph patient reaches in Hora ruled by Kaph	Worsening

11	When the messenger of Pitt patient reaches in Hora ruled by Pitt	Worsening
12	When the messenger of Vaayu patient reaches in Hora ruled by Vaayu	Worsening
13	When messenger binds himself with something, breaks somethings	Bad
14	When Vaidya on way sees good and learned people, girl child, king	Good
15	When Vaidya on way sees king, Cow and calf, mother and child	Good
16	When Vaidya on way sees knife etc.; surgery is expected as a cure	Good
17	When Vaidya on way hears crouch, Ved-Paath, good music, Rains	Good
18	If Vaidya sees or hears of waterbodies in case of Vomit/ Atisaar	Worsening
19	If Vaidya sees or hears of fire, volcano etc., in case of fever, burns	Worsening
20	If Vaidya sees or hears of winds, hurricane case of Gastro issues	Worsening
21	If Vaidya hears words like Stop in case of Atisaar	Good

Some more LakshaN from Sushrut Samhitaa

SN	Risht - LakshaN, specific to Sensory organs. Risht is a proof that body and symptoms are contrary to each other.	Whether Good or Bad
1	When one cannot hear what is being heard by others & vice versa	Bad
2	When one cannot see what is being seen by others & vice versa	Bad
3	When one cannot smell what is being smelt by others &vice versa	Bad
4	When one cannot feel on his skin what normally others can	Bad

5	When one feels a hot thing cold and vice versa	Bad
6	When a good natured man starts mis-behaving	Bad
7	When one cannot feel pinch of a needle or a slap or injury	Bad
8	When one loses taste in mouth or finds opposite tastes	Bad
9	When body smell changes to bad or good without reason	Bad
10	When one is attacked by flies despite a good bath	Bad
11	When one is attacked by birds without any reason	Bad
12	When tongue becomes black and thick	Bad
13	When one's eyebrows/ head show sudden parting of hair (Seeman-tikaa)	Bad
14	One who sees Sun as Moon and Moon as Sun	Bad
15	When suddenly the nose becomes wry	Bad
16	When one is not able to swallow	Bad
17	When one constantly breathes from mouth with struggle	Bad
18	When one is not able to see his own shadow properly	Bad
19	When one remains thirsty despite drinking huge quantity of water	Bad

20	When suddenly black lines come up on patient's forehead/chest	Bad
21	When even pet animals keep away/do not accept from his hands	Bad
22	When urine and excretion increase or decrease without reason	Bad
23	When one cuts his lower lip and licks the upper one constantly	Bad
24	When one perspires heavily in morning hours, more on forehead	Bad

Let us see what Vaagbhat Samhita says about Risht LakshaN

SN	Risht - LakshaN, specific to Sensory organs. Risht is a proof that body and symptoms are contrary to each other.	Whether Good or Bad
1	When a Vaayu patient loses hearing ability	Bad
2	If Patient of Piles starts Shool (painful) in Stomach or Chest	Bad
3	If patient of Dysentery shows/ has unquenchable thirst	Bad
4	If patient has Goosebumps during condition of constant fever	Bad
5	When a pregnant woman starts coughing at the time of labour	Bad
6	When patient breaks wood with wood and iron with iron etc.	Bad

7	When water slips leaving the skin dry	Bad
8	When bleeding starts from any place without any reason	Bad
9	When one feels body limbs very light or very heavy suddenly	Bad
10	When left eye of any patient gets depressed	Bad
11	When Chest gets dry before other parts after bath	Bad
12	When the sputum of patient gets drowned in water	Bad
13	If patient cannot hear heartbeats in ears after pressing ears	Bad
14	When patient's speech is like that of a drunk person	Bad
15	If tears cannot come out of eyes, and person's feet perspire	Bad
16	When pots break, lamp gets extinguished in patient's house	Bad
17	When messenger falls while coming to astrologer	Bad
18	While entering house, if the door, festoons are decorated;	Good
19	If Cows and white Horse are heard or seen in patient's house	Good
20	If astrologer becomes comfortable in patient's house (AC room)	Good
21	If someone from inside politely invites astrologer from front	Good

Dreams as LakshaN

Sleep is one of the biggest riddles for medical doctors. No one has been able to present pathology of how a person falls asleep or how he, naturally, gets up.

About psychological disorders, we need to go by Aapt PramaaN. Much before Sigmund Freud, Charak Rishi has analysed and classified dreams into seven types viz., Drushya (based on what was seen), Shraavya (based on what was heard), Anubhoot (based on what was experienced earlier), Praarthit ((based on what was requested to God), Kalpit (based on imagination say of a film star), Bhaavik (based on what is not related with one's past at all); and Doshaj (based on what has caused by imbalance of Vaat, Pitt and Kaph). Of these, Charak considers only Bhaavik and Doshaj dreams important for diagnosis. The time of dream, if close to Sunrise, shows that it may come true early, and otherwise. Similarly, if person remembers everything and can tell, that narration might be useful in prescribing remedy. This is a big subject, and experience is the only guide. Patanjali has classified Sleep as a Vrittee, a cyclical need of a living being, where the above types of dreams enter due to the above reasons. It is said that sleep is a natural healer, and a person becomes rejuvenated in special way after appropriate sleep.

Sigmund Freud, a medical doctor of Neurosis has also worked on dreams. He says that dream is to take out frustration etc., that could not be physically or socially expressed. It is called Catharsis. He, however, wrote that dreams do indicate certain features about gender. He has categorized that in his opinion, seeing water, a closed room, a table, circular articles like a watch or a clock denote feminine gender; and seeing an odd number, and any weapon or instrument indicate at a male figure! He has said a very surprising thing that dream of a staircase indicates desire to have sex.

For critics of ancient knowledge, it may be the bad news to know that Alexander the Great used to take eminent astrologers with him during war who used to interpret his dreams and advise him about the actions, if needed based on that. One must remember that such historical figures do things which are traditionally acceptable. Simply by denying something, the knowledge does not become redundant. Sleep is a mysterious state of mind and till date no doctors and no scientific research has been able to show that how exactly a person slips into sleep.

It is seen that while we sleep, all organs are closed, excepting our ears; and that ears, as seen in four-footed animals, remain awake for protecting the body. Dogs get up with the slightest noise around so are the cases of herds of cows sleeping in forest. Eyes, lips do not allow their 'food' inside, and unless very significant, skin and nose do not disturb the sleep. Some say that humans can recollect the sound-based memories when they were asleep.

In Vishvakarma Vaastushilp, a book on civil engineering, it is said that if the owner or the king sees in his dream a King's palace, a full moon, rising Sun, a Yajn, boating, horse cart, an umbrella, use of wine in glass, a well-developed tree, an apex of a mountain etc., the project will be beneficial for a longer period. On the contrary, if he has in his dream, a donkey, an owl, a crow, a cat, a buffalo, a valley or a mine, a leafless tree, bursting waterbodies, the result is not likely to be good.

As discussed above, in Ayurved, dreams are said to be a surcharge of Tridosh present in one's nervous and sensory systems, and are classified into seven categories, but only two, as discussed above, are considered as indicative of future. It is said that one should take appropriate actions when in real life things, good or bad, appear as seen in dream. It is said that when one actually vomits the material seen in his dream, though not actually eaten by him that day, it is a certain LakshaN of death within hours. When the dream is independent of any physical inputs, it is to be studied seriously, for example, dreams may show unknown people, unseen deities, strange places etc. The following dreams are considered bad:

1. see dead relatives
2. if one of the shoes is missing
3. entry into a forest (not a garden)
4. wear garland of red flowers and walk
5. drink and enter a party with dead people seen in dream
6. an ugly woman drags toward South direction
7. being bitten or chased by a black dog
8. wearing a red garland
9. ride a buffalo or a pig or a monkey, or a camel, or a tiger, or a dog is indicative of loss or death;
10. a flower or tree growing from any organ of body
11. seeing falling Sun or Moon or see an eclipse
12. eating food as well as the dish; and
13. entering dark abyss or palace.

Good amount of information on dream is given in Sushrut and Vaagbhat Samhitaa on Ayurved, and also in AgnipuraaN to a certain extent, which includes these. These either indicate a death or loss in ventures as the case may be. As against this, seeing a brahmin, professor, umbrella, cows, lions, elephants; eat tasty things, drink likable things, feel the smell of sandal wood or such acceptable smell, and if one sees that one is getting up after falling down: these things show improvement or promotion or awards in the life as the case may be. Famous book named Prashn Gyaan includes Dreams as Omens with reference to change in Ruling authority, Minister etc.

It is said that entire Aitarey Brahman (book related to Ved) was received during a dream! Maybe, it is to indicate that ideas that are stored in our mind for a very long period, suddenly get processed, and are expressed in the dream very clearly. It is a fact that dreams are important part of our mental life and much has been said by Osho on this subject. I have written many lyrics that I, in fact, received in the state of trans, or when my contribution was nil. I have heard many songs that I could not record because the language was not known to me at all. It has happened that I wrote somethings first and then the meaning dawned on me.

Baazi E Badqimaar hai ye zindagi meri
Rahbar mere raqeeb ke paase hain aaine.

A note on Graphology
As we all know that Graphology is a useful science to understand basic qualities and nature of the writer, based on his own handwriting, studying the curves and bars used in Roman script. Today, we see Graphology as a subject, and its reports are admissible in Courts of Law in some cases! It is a new subject and should be used to foretell when needed. I have seen that the height, width and levelled handwritings indicate nature of the writer, even in his absence, and my classmate Shri Prabhakar Shetty could even predict the overall nature, special mental traits of the writer simply based on a random scribbling. If the writing is upward toward the end of sentence, writer is optimistic and vice versa.

The downward strokes and upward strokes indicate confidence depending on stress given there; reasonably rounded letters indicate ornamental qualities; excessively longer bars and rounds indicate dangerous or extremist thinking etc. This science was not there in India, maybe because most of the knowledge was passed on orally, and except for Official documents in the Offices of Kings, nothing needed written evidence. Poetry and drama and some education materials were written on decomposable material like cloth or leaves of trees; and were not important from the point view of preserving as study material; but today, handwritings, per se, have become important particularly regarding social crimes like forgery. Graphology has originated in West based on Roman script that has just 26 letters (inclusive of vowels), written on something; and we need to conduct systematic experiments with the Devanaagari, Telugu and Tamil scripts that, including 12 (popularly known as Barakhadi) to 21 vowels, have more than 55 sounds.

Let us quickly note a few broad features that could be useful in Telegnosis:-
- If the writing is tilted to left, the author is not emotional, and could be introvert
- If the letters are tilted to right, the author is open minded, and extrovert
- If first letter is too big than others, author is interested only in initiating a task
- If loops or letters are overlapping, the author could be hiding something
- If m, n etc. are humped too much, author is emotional and confused in deciding
- If upper and left margins are rather big, author is bold and confident

- If lower and right margins are rather big, author is fearful, having suicidal ideas
- If author makes inner circles in letters like C,G Y, W, he may hide something
- If author makes big canopies on T P etc., it shows self esteem
- Triangular shapes or incomplete in lower zones of Y,G J, show mental disorder;
- Higher upper zones of Y, G, J etc., show enthusiasm of author
- In addition to these, stokes of T, dots on I and J, and Underlines also matter.

We recall that fingerprints were to be admitted as evidence in Courts of Law after the famous case of twins called Harry and Harry; and court decided the situation based on their fingerprints which clarified the matter, and this became a science, even when persons involved in a matter were not physically present. Similarly, so many new LakshaNs need to be admitted into the fold of Telegnosis.

Interpretation, a complex matter
LakshaN may be same but it may give varying meaning from person to person. This happens because every astrologer has his own experience as his guide. Experience builds perception. Perception is more important, and hence each event has different meaning for different people. Thus, the perception becomes important in Telegnosis as to how a LakshaN is interpreted. Suppose I show a photograph of a smiling young woman holding a crying baby in her arms, some think that they are mother and child, some think she is the mother of that baby, some think that it is a baby boy, some say that it is baby girl, some say that mother is taking baby to doctor, and

like that. Like one picture has different interpretation for different people, every Nimitt and LakshaN also has varying interpretation for different individuals. This happens because each one of us has a different set of information in the mind - which causes this variation and therefore prompts differing conclusions. The magic is that each interpretation is a correct answer about genuine questions, if specifically asked.

Nimitt, Shakun (also known as Shagun) and LakshaN refer to external and internal factors, suddenly noted by the astrologer while astrological consultation, that cannot be ignored. All these are perceived through the five sensory organs. It is said that though a blast, a flute, a glass of water, arrival of a person, an invitation, a phone call etc., per se are events and are common to all persons seated in a group but are parts of answer for an astrologer. In a group of astrologers, each of the above events would have differing meaning or connotation or message for each one of them! This is so because each is dealing with a separate question and for each of them, these omens are occurring in different contexts. Further, each astrologer is interpreting it in light of his own set of information. The fact remains that these events would be totally meaningless to those who are not dealing with any question at that time. As said in the other chapter, to note these, it is expected that we practice Traatak and Naad.

Nimitt: It is an event. It could be a sound, some news; a change in visual; a smell; a feeling on skin like a mosquito bite or a drop of oil or eatable on shirt; and a change in taste in mouth. These are the current developments at the site. These, taken individually or jointly, look very simple on the face, but they, when read like an Environmentograph, tell us the answer of a particular question. It is interesting and surprising at the same time. The word Shagun seems to be used as an alternative to Nimitt. For example, seeing a maiden walking to us at the time of going out for a good work is considered as a Good Shagun. A cat crossing your way, particularly from right to left, or someone sneezing or someone saying something against your proceeding for that work etc., are considered a bad Shagun. It is said that if such restrictive Nimitt or Shagun are observed, better to stop for 16 praNayaam, and proceed. If still similar Shagun are seen, better to drop the work for that day. These may not sound practicable in today's busy life. One cannot afford to cancel air tickets and such other arrangements, but still, these Shagun and Nimitt do equip us to be extra cautious about our mission on that day.

LakshaN: This is generally related to external atmosphere and internal changes in physical body (medical issues), this is all related with signs and symptoms appearing in an object or a person (e.g., a patient) that give indications of what is likely to happen. Flowering on a tree can also be a LakshaN. Shakun or Nimitta as has been said elsewhere are generally observed around the place where the question is being dealt with. Let us understand it with some examples. Smoke is LakshaN or indication of some form of fire in that direction. Suppose, eyes of a patient become yellowish, it is LakshaN of jaundice, if the nose becomes dry suddenly or one suddenly starts sneezing, it is LakshaN of some allergy or cold, Vomiting is LakshaN of indigestion etc; and a circle around Moon is LakshaN of good rains in a day or two. Any movement from the right to the left is not considered good because the natural motion of all planets in our solar system is from the Left to the Right! These Left and Right are to be noted with reference to position of the person answering a question based on Telegnosis. These LakshaN become visible when birds fly or when animals move and are deliberately noted by Astrologer. In the same way, when there is abnormally bright sky, prudent people consider this to be LakshaN of some storm etc. and avoid going in that direction.

LakshaN and Water divining

Water divining remains as old an art as human civilisation, because water and rains were always needed for survival. This branch of knowledge is studied as Parjanya Vidyaa. Varah Mihir and Paaraashar are prominent scholars of this branch. Varah Mihir says that depending on vegetation, water can be divined. Similar inferences are possible from texts obtaining in Chapters on Vrukshaayurved in varying books of Ayurved and also in Brihat Samhitaa. Major observations that could be useful in Telegnosis are included here:

1. Water will be just close to surface if there are trees of Nimb or Vat
2. Ample water is possible at barren land because sometimes too much of water discourages vegetation
3. Less heights or short trees indicate waterlogging like situation
4. Branches show a subtle tilt towards the source or direction of the source of water
5. Other things being constant, branches have tendency to grow Northward, if seen with a trained eye
6. Good amount of groundwater is indicated by shining rocks, generally having brown spots.
7. I have read that American army used metallic dowsing-rod, used generally to detect groundwater, for detecting the landmines laid in Vietnam war. This reconfirms that many things can be studied by such LakshaN, based on experience, and save a lot of time and expenditure,

otherwise needed.

8. Touching the urinary organs, eyes, nose, mouth by the querist is generally good for water divining, but places of bad odour and perspiration like armpits indicates bad or non-potable water.

Trees as LakshaN (indicators)

In our own experience, the following conclusions have been true:-

1. Jaamun tree in the 'compound' of the residence leads to severe family disputes and separations
2. One leads lonely and saintly life if there happens to be an Ashok tree in 'compound'
3. A Peepal and a Vat tree in 'compound' kills infants or foetus in the family
4. Family lives in shadow of robbery or theft if there happens to be Imli tree or even its shadow
5. Bilvapatra tree is generally found in 'compound' where at least one child is mentally retarded
6. If some plants are growing in a suppressed portion of 'compound' more so in the South, the family may witness problems in life of children
7. Fruit bearing trees, planted in 'compound' pose barriers in marriage of children
8. If there is garbage caused by vegetation waste etc. in front of main door, it indicates all types of bad-luck
9. The place, where cows and crows assemble regularly, should be selected for residential or business purpose.

LakshaN, and Trees and Rains

1. Rains will be ample for all four months, if birds, more so the crows, build nest near the top of canopy
2. If birds prefer nests in eastern direction of all trees, the

area will receive rains at the end of monsoon

3. Since natural movement of Earth is from left to right, if birds and animals are moving in that direction, it is indicative of a favourable circumstance, and vice versa

4. If birds build nest in North or South, the monsoon will be delayed, and will be less than normal

5. If birds start building nest in Vaayavya, there is no possibility of rains that year.

Shapes of Human organs as LakshaN

LakshaN is something special and other than the normal, that attracts one's attention. Experts say that LakshaN in a human being may relate to his height, weight, voice, gait, skin, complexion, birthmarks etc. Let us take an example, in ancient India, standard height of a person at all stages of life is expected to be equal to 108 times of the middle digit of his middle finger. In another view, the digit is equal to width of toe of a person. All statues for a temple are made in this proportion. Suppose a person's height is 100 digits, or 90 digits, these are indications of medium and undesirable standard, and is considered bad and worse, respectively. For each limb, measurement is specified in books on the subject. The measurement of each limb is stipulated in books on Vaastu Kalaa and in books like Brihat Samhitaa which are observed in building temples and the shrines there. Generally speaking, touching the good organs like head, chest, urinary organs, face, forehead, arm-muscles is considered good with regard to a question. Touching the hair, anus, feet or any depressed part in body (poking nose or ears, naval), feet, nails, teeth is indicative of bad results. Indian LakshaN Shaastra stipulates the following features of human head which can be of instant help to crime detectives.

Head

1. Raised tuft portion indicates a famous but an insistent person,
2. Raised central skull indicates egoistic personality who wants publicity,
3. Raised forehead or temples indicate benevolence of a silent helper,
4. Raised bones above both eyes indicate literary and analytical mind,
5. Raised portion between eyes and ears indicates ability to predict events and vision,
6. Raised forehead between nose and hairline, hints at engineering expertise; and
7. Raised lump above ears are seen in killers and ruthless administrators, but if that portion is suppressed, it indicates miserly traits.

Face

1. Feminine face indicates difficulty in childbirth,
2. Long face shows possibility of poverty,
3. Square face foretells that one could be a thug,
4. Helpless looking people are cruel at heart,
5. A smaller face indicates miserly nature; and
6. If one has hair on shoulders, he may remain poor for a long time.

Nose, Eyes, Ears, Lips

1. A small nose indicates poverty and quarrelsome nature
2. Gums, if seen while a person smiles, show temptation to steal things
3. Suppressed nose indicates undependable person, more so if he has hairy hands
4. Crooked nose shows that the person may be shameless

5. Divided nose-tip shows short of resources
6. Flat nose (excluding racial structure) indicates early loss of spouse
7. Deep eyes indicate miserly tendencies
8. Small eyes show qualities of a military leader
9. and wide eyes indicate good and popular administrator or king
10. Fully red eyes show destructive tendencies and poor health
11. Eyes that have a fine layer of water, indicate ample money and luxury
12. Eyes with too much of water indicates very poor health and short longevity
13. Protruding eyes indicate comparatively less longevity
14. People, who close eyes when they smile, cannot be much trusted for what they say
15. Small and tight lips show miserly tendencies
16. Blackish gums in mouth indicate an instinct to steal others' property
17. If the earlobes are long and heavy, they show gambling activities and abilities to run risks
18. If the earlobes are naturally having small holes, the person may be wealthy and lucky by birth.

Fingers and Toes

We knew one Shri X Jain, (I am deliberately avoiding his first name) a very rich person from Ahmedabad, who left his roaring business of cloth mills, and preferred to be a foreteller to highly placed politicians, businessmen and administrators, even outside India. He always stayed in very costly hotels of Mumbai and had a typical way of foretelling. He asked his clients to be seated before him only in undergarments. He used to offer to client a small chair without hand-rest, placed at a distance of about twenty feet. He used to silently observe the body for good ten minutes and take notes in his notebook. Sometimes he took a round of the client and sometimes the clients were asked to walk a bit and be seated again. While we met him, he was examining photo of a VIP with help of a very big magnifying glass! After he had completed his observation, he told my brother that the person in photo would die in a blast and his head will not be available! And it happened after some months. Let me add one more miraculous observation that he had made with regard to a former prime minister (I am avoiding names for a purpose). Based on the shape of toes of feet of that politician, when he told him that he will be thrown out of the highest seat of Indian democracy, the politician had asked his security to physically lift and throw Shri Jain outside his bungalow. On discussing with him such matters, he revealed that his toes had extraordinarily outward bend.

This reminds that in India, we had a tradition that on arrival of any guest, the guest was required to remove the footwear and then wash his feet. It is said that many predictions can be made based on the shape, colour and print of the wet feet. Based on such things, the host used to have a primary idea of the personality traits of the guest in question. Let us see some of the major LakshaN of feet:

1. The feet should have pinkish shine without any perspiration, if the person is healthy and happy,
2. The toes have dirty, smoky, crooked nails, he will be a poor man,
3. Feet of King, PM, President etc., have very little or no perspiration,
4. Feet with perspiration show some natural disease or some disease is on threshold,

5. A foot raised in the middle indicates constant travelling, and

6. If the blood circulatory nerves are swollen on upper foot, the person could be poor (not necessarily in financial terms, helplessness is a better definition of poverty).

7. If fingers of one's palm are long, he will live life like a King;

8. If the fingers are bent inward with strong joints, he would be a learned man;

9. If the fingers are thin and long, he could be a thinker;

10. If fingers do not bend backward, he may be a physical worker;

11. If fingers are thick at joints, a person may be poor in so many respects; and

12. If fingers are bent backward, the person may die of some weapon.

There are some really good books on Kinesics in English, where they have started compiling the possible interpretation of various gestures made by humans and animals. It may be added that such things are already in our ancient books, like PuraaN. Let us see some of their observations:

- There are 36 styles of movement or gait viz., prowling, plodding, wiggling, strolling etc.
- In a meeting, persons unknowingly keep their toes pointed at the most impressive person; and
- If one crosses legs or arms, the gesture indicates that he is not prepared to accept views readily.

A note on feet

Feet have tremendous capacity to sense. It is said that feet of infants are twenty time more sensitive than ours, and for this reason, the Gynaecologists examine the new born children by touching their feet. Let me connect this also with the Drowsing ability in some people, especially persons with Blood group O Positive. Such people can sense the subtle cold feel when they enter an area with groundwater below their bare feet. Varah Mihir has said that crow and cow prefer to assemble at places where there is ample groundwater below. This is because the feet of animals are naturally sensitive and predictive. Let us recall that no street animals die in any earthquake. Let us be mindful that in earthquake prone areas like Japan, there is a practice to keep an aquarium in each house because the fish, even from thousands of kilometres, and much before the Tsunami has taken place, show restlessness in the glass box. Thus, we observe importance of feet across species.

- Ayurved says that persons who create fluffing noise while walking, are generally patients of Vaayu, such persons are called Sashabdayaataa. If such people leave behind their footprints, some soil or dirt at every step, they may cause exceptionally big loss to family or country.
- When a woman leaves behind her a full print of her wet feet, she is thought to be the best housewife
- If one has naturally dirty or blackish feet, particularly a woman, predict reduced happiness and disorder
- If feet are pinkish or reddish, one has ample wealth and capacity to manage the same. I have seen so many share brokers in Mumbai with this feature
- If a person, particularly a woman, has toes, flat from front, she may not bear child
- If a person has small but reddish toes and nails, he or she might be a commanding king or queen
- Thick toes of both feet indicate need for heavy or menial work for survival
- Persons having hairy knees and ankles are short tem-

pered and unlucky

- If someone perspires with an acceptable fragrance, he should be rich.

Varshaa Vijnaan - LakshaN – Environment

Quite good literature is available in almost all Indian languages that deals with climatic changes, more so for the Monsoon's being favourable or not. In view of this, farmers in India have been following works of Bhadali and Ghaagh. These are being found generally correct. These works depend on Study, testing (PareekshaN), and observations (NireekshaN) of Nature, Vegetation, animal behaviour, and Sky. Junagadh Campus started discussions on Bhadali Vaakya in June 1998, and similar works are undertaken by different campus of Agriculture Universities to use the relevance of those works to foretell daily and average rains in areas of study. Dr. Vaidya, a scientist, made his observations for Gujarat in recent past where he found that predictions, made based on the works of Varah Mihir and Paaraashar, were highly impressive and accurate – just like the ones made by Supercomputer. It is to be understood by us that Supercomputer would depend on Satellite images etc., that can see present scenario (clouds, velocity of wind, direction etc.,) and tell about what is going to happen in coming ten to fifteen days, but on what basis, it will tell us what is going to be the sky like after six months! It cannot tell us; no machines can do that. It is for us to read the nature in its entirety and get signals, and save our lives and plan our agriculture etc. And why not to do that, when the animal kingdom is doing it!

In the seminar held in June 1998, I met many foretellers in the Campus of Junagadh Agriculture University, and I found them to be common men, not having formal technical education of Agriculture etc. They were expert observers of Nature, they heard and saw and smelt Nature the way we are expected to do in Telegnosis. Let us see some major Thumb Rules as follows:-

1. While making a beginning (agricultural operation), if a crow is heard/ sighted/ flies in East, it is good
2. If crows intermittently fly from a direction, there could be a storm coming from that direction
3. When crows bring down their nests, or make new nests close to Stump or lower levels of strong trees, storms could be expected in some days
4. If mango production is good, the monsoon will be less than normal
5. Bumper Ber production indicates good to very good monsoon
6. If Koyal bird (a cuckoo bird) is heard in midnight, good monsoon is expected
7. If crows are heard in midnight, the monsoon will be insufficient or very poor
8. If a white circle is seen around Moon for a long period, good rains are on threshold
9. Wind direction of three main festivals that foretell good or bad monsoon are as given below:-
    - On every Holi, if the wind blows from East and South at the Sunset, Monsoon will be bad;
    - On every Aashaadhi Dviteeyaa, if wind at midday, flows from East, North and Ishaanya, the monsoon will be good or very good, it will be mixed if wind blows from Nairutya; and it will be bad if wind is coming from Agni, South, and West. It is said that if it is coming from Vaayavya, rats or such other insects will cause havoc with the harvest;
    - Another example could be a normal blue sky in win-

ter is no LakshaN, but if it turns orange in morning at 8 a.m. itself, it indicates extreme heat in that region. Such sky is called Deept dishaa and travelling is to be avoided in that direction;

- If at Sunrise of every Akshay Truteeyaa, wind flows from East and Agni, the monsoon will be bad, if wind is from Ishaanya, some pandemic is likely in that area (generally in the radius of ten kilometres); but if the wind flows from West, the monsoon will be good, and very good if from Vaayaavya direction.

Notes

Ayurved & Astrology

Telegnosis, if applied, can be of immense help in the field of health services. It can save substantial money and time for crores of people across the globe. We know that allopathy is doing wonders but is becoming increasingly out of reach of common people even in the developed countries. As a result, handful people in the fields of Pharma and Medical Investigation are in full command. It is not a very good feature of a cultured society. The health services should become more and more affordable if we are to call this world a better place to stay. Anyway, we will make efforts from our side to reduce the time, cost and confusion in this field. Telegnosis has evidently proved of great help in this field, and if more people adopt this, it is desirable, especially when there is no cost on the part of patients.

In a nutshell, let us discuss how Telegnosis proved to be effective. For past decade, many people were covered, most of whom were medically ill for some time, and proper diagnosis was the issue. People used to present their worries and queries to a popular social person, who would summarize the issue over telephone to the astrologer, and the answer, so conveyed did prove helpful either in a changing the medicine, changing the line of treatment, changing the specialist doctor etc., and led to a win-win situation for all, without creating any bad blood. Telegnosis, so far, has served as a second opinion in over 1000 cases; and has been highly appreciated by all parties uniformly and without dispute. Let us remember, that since Telegnosis is principle-based technique, it is applicable to all fields alike.

Ayurved is defined as the science of every form of Life and its longevity. Like miracles made possible in Allopathy, Ayurved has its own unbelievable ways. In Telegnosis, it is our intention to help patients and not to compare these therapies. Pu-Sanvanan Prayog is said to be a victory of medical science over the Nature; The Nasal treatment existed in Ayurved for centuries. Surgical treatment between eyebrows to tackle advanced cases of poisons; chapters are also found as Vrukshaayurved which deal with quick fruiting and growing a tree in palm of a human being; of course, all these could be considered as ornamental; and not the routine treatment. Similarly, there are texts, specific to treatment of domestic animals, and surgery of animals injured in the battle. The intention is to record the available history which says that during RaamaayaN and Mahaabhaarat, SusheN and Sushrut were the chief surgeons in the battle fields, respectively. Let us remember the idol of Bhagavan Ganapati, human body with head of a baby elephant: it does speak of the surgery beyond imagination of modern doctors, even if it is brushed aside by branding it as a mythology!

A brief introduction of Ayurved
About Mahaabhaarat, Sushrut was the chief surgeon and Vaagbhat was the chief medical doctor. From the texts and inference, Vaagbhat seems to be influenced by Charak. He was close to the Paandav side of Mahaabhaarat. Modern historians, under the influence of the West, place Patanjali and

Charak, both between years 400 and 200 BC and for this single reason, many hold a view that Patanjali and Charak are no different persons. It is also said that there exists a very high degree of correlation between the concepts of life and the subtle powers of Life, call it Atmaa, Life, Chi etc. But the fact remains that if Patanjali, the pioneer of Yog was as new as 200 BC, then how come Yog Shaastra (along with Saankhya) is referred to in Bhagavat Geeta, the part of Mahaabhaarat which, according the celestial situations stated therein, dates to October 5621 BC – as mathematically calculated by Dr. Nilesh Oak. I leave this to the prudent readers to decide who is old and who is not, but the fact remains that India had a much systematic understanding of medicines and surgery much before any trace of comparable evidence anywhere other than India. If we go by the latest research, Dr. Nilesh Oak has proved that War of RaamaayaN was fought in the year 12209 BC, and hence the Ayurved, being a branch of Rugved needs to be put much before RaamaayaN. Let us presume that it is about 20000 years before Christ.

In Bhaarat, we believe that this Universe is made of the five basic elements known as Aakash, Vaayu, Agni, Jal and Prithvi; but Ayurved takes three into consideration because for a living being, the Aakaash and Prithvi are constantly available at all points of time and are immobile with reference to his position. In Ayurved, health is defined as maintenance of one's own natural equilibrium of Kaph, Pitt and Vaat (called Tri-dosh): which represent the three Universal elements viz., Water, Fire and Gas, respectively. Ayurved says that each person is born with a proportion of these three. Any imbalance in this equilibrium, caused by any reason, is either a discomfort or a disease. Discomforts due to seasonal changes need not be treated as such, but diseases need to be treated. The definition of cure or remedy is very interesting as it says that any action, any mantra (frequency of sound), any herb or powder, administered carefully in appropriate quantity orally, nasally etc., is the Cure - if it restores the equilibrium as at birth. Ayurved advises separate dose for each patient for same type of disease because every person is born with his individual equilibrium of Tridosh. Ayurved clearly defines LakshaN of Kaph, Pitt and Vayu, and everyone is supposed to know about this, because in ancient India, the school education started with Ayurved. Let me state one small example of this that Kaph, Pitt and Vayu indicate childhood, youth and old age, and also stand for morning, noon and evening, respectively. Eyes were trained to find out LakshaN from the school days, understand the same, and apply the wisdom in real life; all know that Ayurved is replete with inferential knowledge of such LakshaN.

Ayurved treats people in two main ways: Aushadhi and Bheshaj. In Aushadhi, we find preparations and processes to make a medicine of required potency by using herbs and metals to be administered orally, nasally or from eyes, or to be injected into body from some other inlets; and in Bheshaj we include Yajn, Upavaas, Praayashchit, Tapascharyaa, Manoshaanti, Niyam-dhaaraN, Pathyaapathya, Mantra chikitsaa, Daan, Bali (not in the sense of sacrificing animals), Svastyayan (singing praise of God) etc. Such a wide range of treatment is not yet available anywhere other than Ayurved. These ways need to be examined without prejudice because at present, modern medicine men try to find root of every disease inside the physical body. Further, it does not agree at present that some disease could be the result of deeds of past birth. They cannot explain why a person is born blind, deaf, dumb, with more fingers, with two heads, with weak mind etc., For this, Indian sages have shown that these, and also some exceptional conditions like Cancer etc, are acquired by human beings at different stages of life! Agreed that modern medicine explains how a disease is working in a body and what happens when it develops; but they cannot answer that why it happens to a particular person, and that why it is not a general phenomenon! Astrology says that such conditions are rooted in past birth and past karm. Certain examples would come handy. Stealing grain in past birth leads to weak, sick and thin body; stealing and misappropriation of money etc, cause white or black spots on skin; hatred for the noble and respected people leads to headache etc, in this birth; inability to see riches of others bring in problems related to eye-sight.

Ayurved says that there are three categories of diseases, Nij, Aagantu and Maanasaa. Before Sigmund Freud, I think no one bothered for mental disorders which, according to Ayurved, is the major cause of diseases in general. Allopathy is still to take cognizance of diseases emanating from Prajyaaparaadh etc., and remedial measures like Pashchaataap. Maybe it is the question of nomenclature or label. John Woodroffe mentions that 'such labels are a fertile source of confusion about Indian Philosophy'.

Coming back to Telegnosis, the chapters on remote sensing of disease as obtaining in Ayurved known as Doot Shaareer, Vikruti Vijnaaneey etc. deal with diagnosis in addition to the normal ways like asking questions, examination of eyes, tongue, stomach, or any wound or growth. In these chapters, it is specified that what are the certain signs and symptoms of death in some major diseases. It is said that without those signs, death cannot occur in that disease. This area needs to be explored in the interests of humanity. Doot Shaareer deals with the diagnosis of a patient based on examining his representative! Telegnosis is rooted in this concept; and is supported by many books on making predictions.

In astrology, diseases are to be crosschecked based on strength or otherwise of 5, 6, 8 and 12 Bhaav in Kundali for Mental or psychological inflictions (like Evil Eye); physical, and unknown (like being possessed by ghosts etc.) diseases, respectively. The Nij (self) diseases are caused by Kaph, Pitt and Vaayu. Nij diseases at mental level are caused by emotional imbalances (divorce etc.). Aagantu diseases belong to visible and invisible categories. The visible diseases are the ones like COVID which are acquired from others, but the invisible Aagantu diseases and the Maanas diseases emanate from deeds like Prajnaaparaadh and are generally incurable or are as difficult and chronic as Cancer, Alzheimer's. For this type of invisible diseases, astrological advice will be of immense help to the treating doctor.

Ayurved accepts Mantra as a remedy like Dhanurved agrees with Mantra as a weapon. In Dhanurved, it is discussed that the best war is fought by use of weapon-like mantra (Brahmaastra, Krutyaa etc.). As we know, apart from Sanskrit, such remedial Mantra are available mostly in East Indian languages, and in Marathi. Lona Chamaayin is a respected name for her services as a doctor in this sense. We need to note that in today's warfare, the sound frequencies are increasingly being used. It is said that they can break big bridges and huge buildings by creating sound frequencies like the Thunder Whistle, which are not audible to human ear. We already know that we cannot hear even the Dog whistle! Therefore, it is necessary that instead of side-lining or laughing at the use of Mantra, we start learning about its constructive use.

Further, Charak, like said in Saankhya (Yog Sootra of Patanjali are called an Annexure to Saankhya) links diseases to the Basic Five Elements viz, Aakash, Vaayu, Agni, Jal and Prithivi, represented by inputs received and understood through ears, nose, eyes, taste and touch, particularly by a normal adult human being. If any of these organs perceives mutilated communications (Insufficient, wrong and exaggerated), a person can acquire diseases. It is called HeenMithyaati Yog of organs. Let me say that too much of exposure to powerful light or Traatak for long hours is Ati Yog of eye; keeping eyes closed for too long is Heen Yog of eye; and to constantly see from the corner of eye deliberately is Mithyaa yog of eye: This type of disuse of organ causes physical as well as mental disease. For Telegnosis, we need to know these features of Ayurved. Knowledge of these features will also be useful in forming answers in course of the discussions. I have been a witness to some cases where patients behaved abnormally. It was seen that the patients, after committing some wrong to some male or female members and animals, tended to look up, look down or to see from corners of eyes, respectively. I was told that such matters were discussed in chapter on Baal Grah, given by Vaagbhat.

If we see these Samhitaas, and the important PuraaN like Agni PuraaN, VishNu PuraaN and Naarad PuraaN, we find considerable material on LakshaN shaastra with a view to diagnosis and to know about longevity of patients in certain conditions. It means that there were conditions when it was better not to misguide the relatives, who are always prepared to spend heavily to save a patient. We find that these Sages have systematically dealt with the subject by giving certain Thumb

Rules, disease wise and also in general. There are separate chapters in all these three Samhitaas like Vipareetaaviparee-tavijnaaneey, Dootaadivijnaaneet, Vikrutivijnaaneey, Doot-ashaareer. The Sages say that when Risht (the condition not normal and beneficial for that particular person) are seen, the death of patient is almost certain, and the doctor should know it before anyone. Risht is reflected in Roop (outer ap-pearance), Rang (body complexion), Chhaayaa, Prabhaa, Pratichhaayaa (discussed elsewhere), Shareer (Physical body e.g., in a wound), VaaNi (speech of patients), Indriya (the five sensory   organ00000000000000000000000000000000000 and their functions becoming abnormal); and Man (mind).

Ayurved and LakshaN

Ayurved provides good information on Risht LakshaN. It is said that the patients invariably show typical LakshaN before death, and these LakshaN differ in each major disease, listed there in those chapters. It is advised in the books of Ayurved that on seeing these Risht LakshaN, the patient should be treated with utmost kindness and the relatives should be tactfully informed. Expert Vaidya diagnose diseases among healthy persons based on certain LakshaN which are classi-fied as Poorva-roop.

Risht LakshaN - Death as predicted by Ayurved

In Ayurved, it is said that without Risht (LakshaN indicating certain death), no one dies, and hence all doctors are expect-ed to know the general Risht, in addition to disease – specific Risht as detailed in Charak, Sushrut and Vaagbhat Samhi-taa. They have given disease–specific Risht also. The general Risht as indicated by Charak Rishi are as follows:
- getting frequent confusions in normal life
- when the smell or voice of patient suddenly changes

- when his appearance and face become difficult to recognize and smoky
- when his Chhaayaa (aura) changes (Chhaayaa can be seen only by a trained eye)
- when the green coloured fly gets attracted to patient and tries to sit on his lower stomach
- when the patient cannot smell anything good or bad around him
- when he starts suffering from Mithyaa Yog of sensory organs
- when the nose becomes wry
- when the earlobe becomes torn or starts 'hanging'
- when a happy person starts crying and an angry man starts laughing on small things,
- when half side of mouth becomes dry
- when complexion of half body changes
- when suddenly new moles and lines appear on face and neck
- when nails and teeth show a powder like layer
- when lips turn purple
- when capacity to smell is suddenly lost
- when hair become weak and get eradicated just by a small pull,
- when one sees fire in sky
- when flies do not go away from person's body despite applying perfumes
- sudden liking for the things that were not liked earlier, and vice versa,
- when bodily heat is reduced, say if after bath, no other limbs dry except the chest portion,
- when spot between eyes becomes cold, or when a tilak does not dry even after five minutes
- when hair on head become muddy, rough and curled

without any reason
- when body odour suddenly changes
- when the words indicating departure (like Goodbye, see you later, I am going) are heard
- When suddenly there are sounds of blasts or bangs
- When protective articles like an umbrella, shoes, walking stick, spectacles, a cap etc., are seen or heard falling anywhere during the discussion
- when aura around head appears smoky
- when tested medicines do not show impact
- when teeth become dirty without reason
- when a person has strong hic up suddenly
- when the question is asked from South or by facing South direction

General diseases and LakshaN

Ayurved clearly provides major LakshaNs of bodily diseases (Nij) which can be easily or with very little effort, can be identified by Astrologer. If astrologer can observe these features during discussions with patient, this will save a lot of inconvenience on the part of that person. We, therefore, present the following LakshaN as a ready reckoner, subject to ratification by an expert, if disease persists:-

Kaph Rog: The following cause Kaph diseases in general. These diseases generally affect children (like Polio), and trouble is seen to be on an increase during first four hours in morning and in night.

Excessive sleep	Eating fish and Flesh	Excess of Milk products	Common for children
Sleeping during day	Eating calorie rich food	Overeating in general	In Vasant season

More of sweet food	Eating jelly like Jalebi	Excess of fat rich food	First 4 hours of day
More of cold intake	Excess of Til, Sugarcane	Excess of salty food	After 4 hours of Sunset

Pitt Rog:

Following are the most probable causes of Pitt diseases. These diseases influence young persons in general. For example, we generally do not find acidity or Jaundice among children and old people:

Excess of Chilly etc.	Eatables causing loose motions	Eating flex (dried food)	Among young people
Excess of acidic food	Too much anger	Eating without appetite	After monsoon
Excess of liquor	Exposure to heat/ Sun	Eating only salty food	4 hours before Sunset
Excess of garam masala	Excess of shock and fear	Eating in wrong posture	4 hours after midnight

Vaayu Rog:

Because of the following reasons, Vaat diseases come up. These diseases generally are found in old people. For example, knee pain, Alzheimer's disease, dementia, etc. are only rarely found among children and young persons.

Stopping natural calls	Excess of physical work	Excess of fasting	Common for old age
Overeating	Travelling long distance	Exposure to cold (AC)	When clouds come

| Fighting against sleep | Eating dried, acrid food | Ingesting pungent food | Last 4 hours of day |
| Speaking loudly for long | Constant tension, fear | Ingesting chilly food | Last 4 hours of night |

Chhaayaa

In Ayurved, this Chhaayaa word seems to have been used in two ways. Chhaayaa is used to indicate at the aura around a living body, and in Ayurved, it is also used to indicate change in colour of the living body due to medication or reasons relating longevity etc. Many Ayurvedic doctors hold that Chhaayaa refers to the lustre or shine on the skin; which changes according to mood, disease, weakness etc. We all know that before a natural death, patient starts looking different. In such cases, a kind of dust is seen on patients' person, which is nothing but particles of his skin! Thus, he looks as if he is not the same person! Maybe his nose, earlobes, voice, eyebrows, face etc., change or some change occurs in and around his body. Sometimes, some smoke-like presence is also seen around the patient. Traatak and Naad enable us to answer the questions, asked in the process of Telegnosis, and predict unnatural death or accidents.

While the word Chhaayaa has been used in literature to indicate the aura around a living being, the word Pratichhaayaa is the length of his shadow in light of Sun. It is said that sometimes, shadow of certain limbs is not very evident, and that is taken as a bad omen. But we are more concerned with the first which is close to logic for the purpose of foretelling. The second one in related to finding a Muhoort for a particular purpose, and not much is known about it with reference to predictions. We will look into the major aspects of both. There is yet another meaning attached to it and that is Saadhanaa of Chhaayaa Purush, about which we will try to give some reliable information.

Brihat Samhitaa interprets Chhaayaa as Lustre on the skin. It poetically says that the Lustre is comparable to the shining walls of a metallic pot in which a lamp is burning. It accepts that the body is made of the Five Elements viz., Aakaash (Ether), Vaayu, Agni, Jal and Prithivi (Earth); and it says that one of these is always a prominent feature of a living being; and a trained eye can 'see' that. It is said that the following features give primary indication of prominence of these elements in a person:-

- If Aakaash Element is prominent, one will be intelligent, grammarian, fearless,
- If Vaayu Element is prominent, one will be thin, moody, quick moving,
- If Agni Element is prominent, one will be energetic, thin, good eater, cruel,
- If Jal Element is prominent, one will like to swim, frequently thirsty; and
- If Prithivi Element is prominent, one may be a great admirer of perfumes etc.

Chhaayaa as a tool of foretelling:

Coming to the information about Saadhanaa of Chhaayaa Purush, it is again related with extending the sensing capability of human mind. In this, a person is required to meditate on his own shadow of almost his size on a clean white wall in a dark room by lighting a lamp behind him. He should sit on an appropriate table etc., to cause such a shadow. He should constantly focus on the shadow at the point where his eyebrows would have met. It is expected that after some months, the person is able to see his shadow very clearly even during the day light. Then he is able to move it or even transport it at a desired place; this enables him to know whatever he wants to know from that place. That place could be a marriage party, a place on Moon or Mars. The distance does not matter for the Chhaayaa to travel; in fact, it is believed to be the extension of the Saadhak himself. I know about two such incidents where one person was seen at two places simultaneously. At this stage, if the saadhak is not able to see feet or stomach of his own Chhaayaa, or if both hands are not seen, saadhak comes to know that his own death is not far; if he does not see his right hand, loss of brothers can be predicted; and loss of wife is predicted if the left hand is missing in Chhaayaa for a longer time.

It is added that even after the death of a human being, his Chhaayaa could be traced if his body is available. That is one main reason that Hindu cremate the dead bodies. It is said that after the atomic disaster in Japan, Chhaayaa of many trees and buildings were visible to naked eye in the form of slowly dismantling particles. We all know that though the person is declared clinically dead, his organs are good for transplantation if removed within 4 hours of his death, and are properly preserved. In the same way, human existence is likely to be traced for some hours or days, after his death because Ayurved says that if dead body is kept for a longer period, Dhananjay Vaayu takes up process of decomposition of body which, in some definite ways, is extension of existence in yet another form; and communication with those decomposing particles or even to the ex-owner of that body, is possible until the body is destroyed. Maybe tomorrow, some machines will be made to sense those particles. Scientists, who work on Tissue culture, would not laugh at these possibilities.

We find reference to Prabhaa, Chhaayaa and Pratichhaayaa, which need to be understood while discussing Telegnosis as related to treatment of patients. These are typical words used in Indian medicine. Prabhaa is the word used for energy in the body, in any form, which causes an aura around body which is available to Kirilian camera etc., and also to the trained eyes which is called Chhaayaa. Hunting animals identify dead bodies due to their ability to see this Prabhaa from a distance. The physical shadow or image, visible to all of us in Sun-light, water or mirror etc., is called Pratichhaayaa. All living beings invariably have Prabhaa, and hence Chhaayaa too.

Chhaayaa afflicted or influenced adversely by Vaayu becomes smoky or pinkish more so around the weaker part of patient's body; if influenced by Pitt, Red colour is seen; in case of increase in Water element in body, the Chhaayaa shows dark blue sheds; if affected by Earth or Prithivi element, light blue aura or almost white colour is said to be present around the affected limb of a person; and if Aakaash or Etheric element is affected, the Chhaayaa shows light blue aura appearing around entire body of patient. Any disturbance, external or internal, mental or physical, immediately impacts the Chhaayaa, and a trained Vaidya gets help in his diagnosis. In Jain philosophy, it is said that the past deeds keep approaching the person, and apart from diagnosis, the Vaidya or a Muni, can foretell an event even in the distant future. They call it Leshyaa.

Lamp Analysis

This is very important and old method practiced in many parts of India. Many do this just as a routine during their daily meditation, but in fact, this is a handy method to know the result of a task on hand. In India, we light a lamp at the beginning of every good work, function, journey, program; and all are expected to observe the flame. In fact, no one knows that the flame needs to be observed. Today, it is treated as an offering to the deity, the astrological part, easily available, is often missed. I have been seeing for over 60 years now, and I find that the indications given by the flame are a very great help every time. The subject is beyond words and hence, we can only discuss this by citing some illustrations which will immediately enable us to learn it. On seeing the following table, one will easily understand how nicely our ancestors have developed this science, of course, modern laboratory-based education has taught us to ignore such aspects.

Here, internal fuel (ghee or oil) shows the good or the bad, the internal will to perform, naturally available to querist; the wick indicates longevity and represents the body of the querist (for example the wick may be short, long, dirty, intertwined not well placed etc.); the external fuel is air or oxygen in atmosphere which indicates how much support the environment is prepared to give; and Jyoti, the Flame (the end result of all these factors) shows how strong or weak is the net position of the querist, at present. In other words, if enough Ghee is available in lamp, the person is willing to perform; If wick is short, maybe the person is enthusiastic, but due to destiny, the program may not last long; If flame burns violently for any reason, the interpretation is that the surrounding factors will adversely affect the Mission; and lastly, if the Flame is bright and long, the program will run impressively (for a shorter period if the wick is short).

If Lamp / Flame	Result
Burns with cracking sound sparks emitting out	Bad (more so about a patient)
Is very small and dull	Bad outcome
Has less oil support	Less longevity (due to internal strength)
Shows something floating in oil	Infection, poison, external interference
Is long and normal	Good and quick results
Very long and shakes	Good for a short period
Shakes violently without wind	Bad results
If wicks are intertwined	New symptoms, new enemies/ friends
If someone puts on fan to extinguish lamp	Conspiracy, bad outcome, external evil

Direction of the Flame and its movement

If burning Flame	Result
Generally, turns to East	Good
Generally, turns to Agni (SE)	Bad due to various fears
Generally, turns to South	Bad to very bad and death
Generally, turns to Nairutya (SW)	Bad and indicative of devilish mental disorder
Generally, turns to West	Good and indicative of successful treatment

Generally, turns to Vaayavya (NW)	Bad due to expensive methods
Generally, turns to North	Good and shows victory
Generally, turns to Ishaanya (NE)	Overall good

I have successfully tried this method in many Vaastu Prashn. I use incensed stick or a small lamp/ candle to see the direction of smoke/ flame in a closed room on the Site of ready-made flat or office or residence etc. I have seen that whenever the flame or smoke goes south, the previous owners did have issues relating to profitability. Sharp turn toward South, strongly indicates presence of invisible powers, occupying the place; and may cause some problems to the people who want to stay or perform at that place. Bright flames have always confirmed good results with regard to health and wealth.

It is suggested that astrologers request the querist to light lamp before giving the final answer.

Notes

Svar Shaastra

This is the most secular science that deals with PraaN (breath) and many Yogi have attained spiritual heights only because of control and knowledge of PraaN. This area has always remained beyond the reach of Ayurvedic/ medical scholars; and is too new for Allopathic doctors. In other words, no one has been able to explain why we breathe from one nostril at a time though we have two. There is also no answer as to why some animals have two nostrils and what is its advantage over the animals and birds like sparrow who have no nostril, or who breath from mouth!

Researchers seem to be baffled by variety of species created by Nature. What is so good, logical and desirable that humans have two nostrils, two eyes, two ears, as many as five fingers in palms and feet, and that too they differ in size! If security was the purpose, why even a single eye is not part of our Anatomy? Such questions might sound too theoretical and unnecessary, but such are the ideas that inspire medical doctors to resort to spiritual pursuits.

In view of the above, it is advisable for us to go by what is said by Sages. Unless we study and experience this science, there will not be any room for decoding the mystery. We, therefore, should start from where they left. The wisdom available in this area is summarized below for a ready reference. It is agreed that it is too short of needed explanations, but such is this boundless subject, presented in a few Sanskrit books. Shiv Svaroday, Pavan Vijay Svaroday are the two main books on this subject, while Shiv Svaroday, having 395 Shlok on over 90 areas of concern, is easily available in market, Pavan Vijay is not. Apart from these, this is believed to be a subject that is directly taught by a Guru to his disciple and knowledge, together with words of first-hand wisdom, passes on in the form of oral tradition. Almost all sects in India, Sanaatan, Sikh, Jain, Bauddh, Naath, Yog have been having high regard for the usefulness of this Science in their Saadhanaa. This is yet another feature of Indian Knowledge System which is believed to be independent of any other branch of astrology, Tithi, Vaasar, Muhoort, Hora etc.

In our body, we have two nostrils and we breath in and out from the time of birth till death. It is said that generally a person breathes 21800 times per day, and if everything remains favourable, he may live for 100 years! This is further analysed that in a standard healthy body, one nostril works for one Hora (which is equal to 2.5 Ghati). The English word 'hour' seems to have been evidently derived from this measurement unit of time. It is specified that there are 24 horas in an Ahoraatra (one day). The seven major planets are said to be the Lords of Hora. It is said that when our Solar system came into existence in the Universe, first Hora was ruled by Sun, followed by Hora of (each of 2.5 Ghati) Shukra, Budh, Moon, Shani, Guru and Mangal. When we keep counting Hora in this order, the twenty fifth Hora is the first Hora of the next day. For this reason, India specifically called it 'Saptaah' (Made of seven days). The word 'Week' does not show anything per se, but still follows this order, origin of which, is in Svar Shaastra of India.

In Svar Shaastra, Left and Right nostrils stand for Moon and Sun, and the transition period is ruled by Agni. Agni is the Supreme God, it is because of Agni that any temperature is caused, cold or hot, as exists in Sun and Moon. According to the meaning of Svar as interpreted in Hathhayog, the exhaling (H) is Sun and inhaling is Moon (Thh); or it represents Shiv and Shakti. Svar Shaastra has gone a step ahead of Ayurved in this context and has tried to assign areas to Idaa and Pingalaa Naadi. While Idaa indicates female and feminine objects; the Pingala indicates the opposite. One major reason for such specialisation could be the fact that feminine species conceive and protect the foetus, for which the Mother Nature has given them appropriate patience and defence mechanism. This difference must be present even on the first day after the female foetus was conceived in womb. It is also seen that survival rate of female children is higher even under adverse situations as compared to the male children. The works of Jeevak Kaashyap, the medical officer in the Court of Bhagavaan Buddh, are the best on women specific diseases; and Nepalese area is impacted by him.

It is not proper and logical to say that Svar Shaasta is a branch of Jyotish because nowhere it is so established; but Sages have shown that its use in Social matters is equally effective as in Spiritual matters. It is seen from the text that it agrees that the visible world has evolved itself from the five Elements and it will get back to that form after the process is over. This it seems to be in tune with Saankhya Darshan of Bhaarat. It, however, is to be reiterated that this is the Mother of all Sciences, and it is added that an astrologer without knowledge of this Science, is incomplete. It comes as a surprise for the atheists. Yogi seem to be using this for exploring the secrets of Universe by doing Saadhanaa in appropriate Hora, divided further into Five elements, ruled by Vaayu, Agni, Earthen element, Water and Aakaash in that order. Each of this, rules the breathing for 8, 12, 20, 16 and 4 minutes in that order, thereby making one complete Hora. If this is true for some yogi, his side of breathing will change every hour, commencing from Sun-rise. It is added that such hourly change in breath is possible only in a standard healthy body, hence each of us must first study our average time of change in breathing from each nostril; and work out the flow of each of the above five elements accordingly. I find that the average time per nostril differs in each individual depending on his health, mood, age; and mostly is in the range of two to three hours! Normally, Svar changes with urination, bathing, and with any sudden change in posture.

Svar Shaastra recognizes existence of the Five elements, as listed above, in every living body system. Our Man, the Mind, is a kind of place where ideas, perceptions, impressions, memories etc., reside in some form - virtual or physical or in any other way. We do require a garage to park a car, a road to drive it, a mechanic to know its composition and to repair it in case of need: If a car is a reality, the garage and the road and the mechanic do co-exist. Thus, our mind is a reality, however inexplicable and invisible it may be. This is known and respected as Aakaash Tattv in body of any animal. The active nervous system could be called Aakaash. It could be compared with a road or a garage which are used by thoughts etc. Similarly, the Vaayu, is the power to move anything. It transports thoughts and ideas and sensations inside the body, and it is the power due to which objects can be pushed or pulled in physical world. Agni is the element due to which we are able to digest food inside the body, and it is reflected as energy that converts forms of matter: if we remove heat from Water, it turns into solid ice, and if we add Agni to it, it rises as visible vapor and then slowly becomes part of the gaseous and invisible sky. Water is to be understood in similar way. The Earthen element is the most consolidated and visible and palpable of all the five elements. Our bones are made of such solid matter. Such is the philosophy of five forms of Matter as preached by Svar Shaastra. After providing such analytical ability, Svar Shaastra leaves us at the door of Guru to understand role of Atmaa, the power who administers these five forms of Matter!

Svar Shaastra tells us that PraaN and Mind both are interdependent, and together, they could be called Atmaa. PraaN is nothing but vibrations of Mind (Yog Vaasishth). The one who knows either of these two, knows or can know everything in Universe. It is for this reason that we consider Svar Shaastra important from point of view of Telegnosis. While dealing with features of PraaN, that resides in these Naadi like Idaa, Pingalaa, it is said that it has ten main features:
- Activity (ability to act and react);
- Absence of physical matter of Five elements (It is neither Shabd, nor smell etc., Panch Tanmaatraa);
- Nishkaasan or Dvesh (because of this feature, one person does not readily accept or reject views of others, and maintains individuality);
- Mano-bandh-kaaritaa (it is due to this that PraaN acts as per analytical advice of his own mind, and not others, in other words, it has its own thinking power);
- Vistaarita (PraaN wants to extend its areas of sensing and influencing. Many scientists have started believing that a man wants to know more and more, and is never satisfied

even with complete information);

- Aajnaakaaritaa (PraaN goes by alternatives offered by mind, and does not go outside it. It is like the President of a country, who ultimately follows what the democratically elected Prime Minister says);
- Aprasupti (PraaN is never inactive);
- Shram-Raahitya (PraaN is never tired of actions);
- Sankraatmakataa (it wants to communicate with other forms); and
- Viraam – Gatitv (It acts then takes rest and then again acts).

It is said that there are many Naadi (cobweb of nervous system) in human body, among which there are ten main ones, and of those ten, the Pingalaa, Idaa and SushumNaa are the three most important for Yogi and Astrologers. Since the subject is an ocean, we will first see certain facts, tabulated below, that will help us in understanding the subject, read with the other chapters, especially the Chapter on LakshaN.

	Breath in Right Nostril	Breath in Left Nostril	Transition period
Planet	Sun	Moon	Rahu
Naadi/ Nostril	Pingalaa	Idaa	SushumNaa
Nature	Ugra/ Angry	Saumya/ Sober	Unpredictable
Element	Pitt (Heat energy)	Kaph (Coolness)	Vaayu (gaseous)

There are a good number of hymns in different Sanskrit books which can be referred to if needed, but the following information will suffice for the purpose of application of Telegnosis.

Feature	Pingalaa (Right Side)	Idaa (Left Side)	SushumNa (both sides)
Gender	Male	Female	Neutral
Deity	Shiv (Shankar, Father)	Shakti (Parvati, Mother)	Eunuch
Complexion	Black and Dark	White and Light	Like smoke
Time	Day - presence of Sun	Night - absence of Sun	Twilight/ Transition
Ruling element	Agni and Vaayu	Earth and Water	Aakaash
Speed	Fast, Mobile	Slow and Steady	Cannot predict
Weekdays	Sun, Tues, Saturday	Mon, Thurs, Friday	Wednesday
Lunar date	Dark Half 1, 2, 3, 7, 8, 9, 13, 14, 30 Bright Half 4, 5, 6, 10, 11, 12	Bright Half 1, 2, 3, 7, 8, 9, 13, 14, 15 Dark Half 4, 5, 6, 10, 11, 12	Not applicable
Raashi	1,4,7,10	2,5,8,11	3,6,9,12
Direction	East and North	West and South	NE, SE, NW, SW
Location	Below, Behind, Right side	Upward, in front, left side	Not applicable
Number	Odd 1,3,,5,7 ….	Even 2, 4, 6, 8 ….	Not applicable

It is stated that the following table would be very useful for all astrologers:-

SN	Advisable when Right nostril works	Advisable when Left nostril works
1	While physical work/ instant result	Starting Sober things for long term results
2	Learning operation of weapons	Making efforts to befriend someone new
3	Daily study of books	Going to temple or Yajn or Poojan of God
4	Coitus	Start building a temple etc.
5	Making a machine/ a Yantra (tantra)	Start a religious movement
6	While meeting administrators	Start a work for mass benefits
7	Court cases, battle field	Initiate marriage proposal
8	While taking bath or cleaning bowels	Enter the newly built house
9	Ingesting food and taking a sleep	Lay the Foundation stone of a structure
10	At daily exercise or wrestling	Commence work of a new well, garden etc.
11	While taking or giving medicine	Discuss new business ventures
12	Riding the vehicles	Plan and execute the map of a new town
13	Climbing a tree or a mount	Sow seeds in an agricultural field for crop
14	While taking a boat journey	Start medication for rejuvenation (Kalp)

15	While attending office as a servant	Commence journey for a distant place
16	While swimming	Propose marriage or friendship
17	While taking liquor or such drinks	Sing prayers etc.
18	While gambling	Go for gatherings of friends and family
19	On a hunting operation in forest	Attend welcome ceremony of King/ Officer
20	Starting a difficult Saad-hanaa	Take oath on promotion etc.
21	Starting Saadhanaa of an angry God	Conserve food, clothes etc. for needy class
22	While doing exorcism	Wear the new clothes
23	While applying hypno-tism etc.	Open a new pharmacy
24	While actually buying a property	Attend or perform music and dance
25	While actually selling a property	Take up pilgrimage
26	While opening a new leaf in books of Accounts	Start good Saadhanaa or a Mantra
27	During a talk on busi-ness expansion	Make donations and pay dues to others
28	While actually writing a letter	Planning a work, Meeting new employer
29	While cutting diamonds etc.	Ingest cold drinks and take liquid food
30	While holding talks with competitors	Start treatment of a diffi-cult patient

| 31 | While entering home on return | While proceeding from home for work |
| 32 | While taking up short journey | While starting long journey |

In Svar Shaastra, we also find excellent guiding principles to start our day. There are two methods given here, the first gives stress to weekdays, and the second is focused on Tithi, or Lunar Date. As we saw, it is believed that it was Hora of Sun, when the first day commenced on our Planet Earth, but we do not know for ourselves that such was the fact; but the other method based on Tithi, is an arithmetical truth because we know the exact position of Sun and Moon, every minute. I am inclined to follow Day system as per this Shaardool-aveekridit in Prashn Marg, giving a Thumb Rule:-

If breath at Sunrise, happens to be	Result (for avoiding the following trouble)
On Sunday in Left Nostril	Body pain due to some reason
On Monday in Right Nostril	Quarrel with some person
On Tuesday in Left Nostril	Death or such fatal accidents, injury
On Wednesday in Right Nostril	Failure in journey/ business / discussion
On Thursday in Right Nostril	Trouble from Administrators or Royal offices
On Friday in Right Nostril	Nothing may be favourable
On Saturday in Left Nostril	Loss in business & arguments

Similar Thumb Rule is also given with regard to Tithi, please note the following:-

	Shukla Paksh (Bright) Left Nostril	KrishN Paksh (Half) Right Nostril
Good	1,2,3,7,8,9,13,14, Poornima	1,2,3,7,8,9,13,14, Amaavasyaa
	Shukla Paksh Right Nostril	KrishN Paksh Left Nostril
	4,5,6,10,11,12	4,5,6,10,11,12
Bad	If opposite is seen at Sun-rise	If the opposite is seen at Sun-rise

It is written by the Sages that within each Hora, the five elements get reflected, and if noted properly, the same could be of great use while making predictions. Let us see the same in the table. Astrologers should make efforts to know which Tattv is flowing in his breath, whether from Left or Right. For the present, let us assume that his breath is well in tune with the healthy body, and that his breath changes with change in each Hora of 60 minutes (2.5 Ghati, as said above).

Feature	Minutes	Length of breath	Colour/ shape/ Speed
Vaayu	8	Breadth of 8 digits	Blue/ Round shape/ fast
Agni (Fire)	12	Breadth of 4 digits	Red / Triangle/ Steady
Prithivi (Earth)	20	Breadth of 12 digits	Yellow/ Square/ Steady

Jal (Water)	16	Breadth of 16 digits	White/ Half circle/ Fast
Aakaash (Ether)	4	Unpredictable	Mixed/ Irregular shape
TOTAL	60 min / Hora		

To be still more certain of the flow of breath in a particular element, some astrologers keep five marbles of the above colours, and take out one from the pocket to confirm the running element. Such crosschecking is not only necessary but over a period of time, it steps up the confidence of Astrologer in the Astrology as a divining tool. It is indeed very surprising that how suggestive and vocal the environment around us is! We often mistake these eloquent indications as superstition. I suggest that let us first study what the Sages have studied before rejecting the same.

Extending the interpretation, it is seen that since Agni and Vaayu are highly moveable, predictions need to be made with this in view: Here also, Agni indicates upward movement and Vaayu shows lateral movement. In case of Water as element, the movements are very slow and are downward, but in astrological Kundali, the watery Raashi like Kark, Vrushchik indicate quick movement, especially if in Aaroodh or Lagn. The Earth shows slow and circular movement not very clearly felt (let us see that while Ayurved deals with three of the five elements viz, Kaph, Pitt and Vaayu; Astrology goes ahead and includes the forth viz, Prithvi Tattv also). In Human body, Agni Tattv is more prominent in Shoulders, Vaayu in abdomen, Earth rules the loadbearing legs and knees, Water rules the excretory systems and bodily travel due to both feet;

and Aakaash Tattv rules the thinking system or nervous system. Sages advise us to initiate hard work when breath flows in Right nostril with sub-flow of Agni and Vaayu; and initiate long term good missions when breath is in Left with sub-flow of Jal (Watery) or Earth elements. When the Sushum-Naa is expected to run, better to pray selflessly: I have seen that social prayers bring damaging results when answers are given in SushumNaa Naadi.

Some more Thumb Rules are given below which are illustrative in nature:-

- If some task is initiated when breath is in Left and Water segment is flowing inside, the work will be a success for decades and will be functional very soon (within a year or so!) – If it is a patient, he will recover soon; if a case of pregnancy, the woman may get a daughter;
- If some task is initiated when breath is in Left and Earth segment is flowing inside, the work will be a grand success for very long period and will be functional in near future (with some delay or as per the schedule) - if it is a marriage , there will not be divorce; if a case of pregnancy, the woman may get a healthy son;
- If some task is initiated when breath is in Right and Agni segment is flowing inside, the good work will be soon over but there may be some areas of dissatisfaction – a person, though highly placed, may soon be transferred for not maintaining quality; if a case of pregnancy, the woman may deliver a child (mostly a son) but after some complications; and
- If some task is initiated when breath is in Right and Vaayu segment is flowing inside, the good work initiated will get washed away soon; the project may get destroyed or abandoned; if a case of pregnancy, the woman may

have abortion of female fetus.

Aakaash is not a good element in breath for normal social situations, hence let us summarise the result of the other four elements, running in our breath with some typical areas of questions, normally asked to astrologers:

Area of questions	Pruthvi	Jal	Agni	Vaayu
Disease	Slow, good	Quick good	Not good	Prolonged
Child birth	A baby boy	A baby girl	A baby boy	A baby girl
Marriage	Yes, good	Very good	Not good	Separation
Traveller	Ok, delay	Coming	May be sick	Unhappy
Travel	Good one	Success	Not good	Troubles
Guest	Welcome	Good meet	Not good	Loss giver
Business	Slow gains	Buy for gain	Not good	Volatile bad
Lost thing	Get in East	Get in West	Lost in South	Lost in North
Agriculture/ Water	Good	Better	Insufficient	Bad quality

We present a bird's eye view in a tabular form as shown below as a ready reckoner for beginner:-

Idaa Naadi (Left Nostril)	Pingalaa Naadi (Right Nostril)
Female, feminine articles	Male and masculine articles
Good for new friendship, marriage, work	Good for routine matters
Indicates Anti clock wise movements	Indicates Clock wise movements
Rules the frontal or foreground scenario	Rules the scenario behind/ background
Relates to predictions internal to any matter	Deals with matters external to a matter
More related with Water & Earth elements	More indicative of Vayu and Agni elements
Sober in nature	Rough in behaviour
Rules over Left side of body	Rules over Right side of body
Can be called equal to Yin in Chinese	Can be called equal to Yang in Chinese

On the one hand, we have empty-handed saints and Sages and doctors, providing free service to sick, and on the other, we have professional service providers charging huge fees! These professionals often fail to know many basic things about a patient, more so if their instruments do not support them. They feel paralyzed if they do not have past history, pathological and radiological reports etc. It is not that we should be against such technological advancement, we are just trying to show how dependent they are on machines. It is felt that in such situations, Svar Shaastra comes to help.

Ayurved and Svar Shastra do explain the use of each nostril

in humans. I have seen scholars of Ayurved suffering from an inferiority complex. There is one valid reason that scholars of Ayurved have been lagging in presenting their strong points like Nasya Chikitsaa, Dhoom Chikitsaa, Rakt Moshan (allowing some blood out), Mantra Chikitsaa, Naadi Pareekshaa, Doot Shaareer. With some more research and personal interactions, one can see success of most of these chikitsaa from one's own eyes.

After some months of practice of aforementioned summary, it is certain that one will be able to foresee many things, and it is, therefore, felt that if the predictions are made with support of the other chapters in this book, one will be well-versed in guiding society in many ways. It is suggested that astrologer may use this knowledge in light of LakshaN and Aaroodh Lagn!

Notes

Ank Shaastra (Indian Numerology)

The subject happens to be vast and can be compared with the knowledge in the West in many ways. But as said earlier, here in Telegnosis, we are taking its help as one of the tools and hence we will confine ourselves to its major aspects and shall avoid the finer details. In India, we do not use zero and nine as part of numerology. It is confined to the major seven planets and the referential point called Rahu (thereby omitting Ketu). Each is assigned a number as shown below where we show their nature and area which they represent. It is also referred to as Ashtamangal as it has eight number.

No.	Planet	Body mechanism	Element represented
1	Sun/ Soorya	Bones	Pitta
2	Mangal	Muscles	Pitta
3	Guru	Fat	Vaayu
4	Budh	Skin	Vaayu
5	Shukra	Reproductive system	Kaph
6	Shani	Nervous system	Vaayu
7	Chandra	Blood	Kaph
8	Rahu	Feet	Like Shani

Numerology and methodology

The querist is asked to write or indicate a number, having three digits of his choice. Suppose, he says 123; the first digit represents the past (about the question), the second digit '2' stands for current position; and the third digit indicates future. The first, second and last digit also represent Head, Middle body and body lower than abdomen. If the question is asked with reference to some sickness, the astrologer can infer that person is affected by heat or fever with headache (because 1 indicates Sun, Pitt and Head); and perhaps entered the second stage of that disease which has shifted from his bones to muscles with general fever (because 2 indicates Mangal, Pitt and muscles); and that the remedy will come soon (due to Vaayu indicated by '3' as third digit). The doctor would be a tall, fat and healthy person (as '3' is ruled by Guru).

Suppose someone selects a typical number like 222, 333, 111 etc., it is either to be ignored or to be interpreted as indicative of no change in the situation, at lease without major changes. It can be added that the champions of this method, divide the selected number by 30,27,12,9,7 and 5 to arrive at the remainder to be taken as important and relevant lunar tithi, nakshatra, Rashi, planet, day and Basic Element like Fire, Water. Let us leave these calculations for those who want to develop this method.

Note

One can experiment and connect the other finer details to enrich the literature, but here we are simply using this to crosscheck our prediction based on Svar, LakshaN, Aaroodh etc.

Sound of Question (Prashnaakshar)

We have already seen the origin of thoughts, sound and language in a chapter given earlier in this book. It is suggested that we may relate the following with those concepts. It is added at this stage that today we are dealing with questions over audio and video telephone, and for this reason, this chapter becomes still more relevant. This approach also becomes relevant when language of the querist is not known to the astrologer. Prashn Gyaan also includes this in its last chapter and recommends this technique for any questions asked after Sunset.

Prashnaakshar: This means the consonants or vowels used in the language of question. This becomes more important when the astrologer does not know language of querist. In Sanskrit, the sounds are measured as Laghu and Guru (Short and Long syllable) and Indian Prosody (Chhand shaastra) deals with eight units of three letters each, called GaN which are Ya (122), Ma (222), Ta (221), Ra (212), Ja (121), Bha (211), Na (111), and Sa (112). Each GaN is assigned to the Seven planets and to Rahu. To see an example of Ja Gan, we can take the word 'Ashok', Mohan is the example of Bha Gan. Here, 1 is used to show Laghu and 2 is used to show Guru Maatraa.

It is inferred that if the question starts with any one of the 21 vowels (17 vowels like a, aa; I ,ee; u, oo; e, ai; O, Au; Hru, Hroo; Lru Lroo; Um, Uh, Aum and 4 imported from Persian and English usages), the result is expected to be good; and if it starts with a consonant, the result would depend on the GaN to which it belongs. In general, a question starting with Ya, Ma, Bha, and Na GaN fetch good results. Vowels, called Svar in Sanskrit, indicate Life or longevity, and each consonant shows different type of audio-body. Vowels are the sounds produced by man without use of lips, tongue, teeth, palate; it is just the exhaling of breath in different ways. In consonant, the PraaN is activated to produce consonants by active use of palate, tongue, teeth, and lips. Most of the animals are able to produce vowels to varying extent, but consonants seem to be specific to human vocal system. Sages have assigned GaN to different Elements, Raashi, Sun and Moon; and this helps in firming up our answer to a specific question. in Telegnosis, we try to answer the same question in different possible ways and by using easy methods. It is something like an object, kept in the centre of a room, being seen from windows in walls on all sides. The following table may help us in ascertaining which Planet is ruling the question, based on the first cluster of three consonants:-

Prashnaakshar (First part of Consonant cluster)	Indications (Element, main feature)
Ya GaN (122)	Watery/ Raashi like Kark, Meen, General good
Ma GaN (222)	Earth/ Raashi like Vrushabh, General riches
Ta GaN (221)	Aakash/ Emptiness, Poverty etc.

Ra GaN (212)	Agni/ Raashi like Mesh, Energy, Heat, Arguments
Ja GaN (121)	Sun God/ Administrative matters, add to energy
Bha GaN (211)	Moon God/ Mother, Sukh, family, Increase in liquid etc.
Na GaN (111)	Svarg (General happiness), the best GaN
Sa GaN (112)	Vaayu/ Raashi like Kanya, Movements, travels

While the above classifies consonants into GaN, the following table indicates different clusters of consonants, classified in Varg (cluster), ruled by the eight planets. This classification becomes particularly useful where taste is to be identified as often required in Bhojan Prashn and Koop Prashn. Suppose a question is asked with K as the first consonant, the taste of water of will be acrid or Kashaay because the question is ruled by Mangal, as tabulated below:-

Prashnaakshar	Ruling deity/ Feature	Taste/ Type of result
Any of 17-21 vowels	Moon, General good	Kshaar,Salty,General good
S SH H	Sun, Admn, Father	Acidic (Ketu),
K Kh G Gh	Mangal, brother, support	Toora and Tikta (Kashaay)
Ch Chh J Jh	Budh, Intellect	Mixed
T Thh D Dhh N	Guru, Divinity	Sweet
T Th D Dh N	Shukra, Beauty, riches	Sour

P Ph B Bh M	Shani, Wisdom, slow	Tikta TeekshN (Pungent)
Y R L V Sh	Y R L V Sh	Tasteless

It is added that Chandra and Soorya have only Raashi but in the above the other have two each: Mangal will Rule K and Kh under Mesh; and will Rule G and Gh under its other Raashi named Vrushchik; and like that Budh, Guru, Shukra and Shani are also given the Sounds falling in Raashi that they rule. Normally, in India H falls under Kark ruled by Chandra, but in this branch of astrology, H is ruled by Soorya! In India, such ideological difference is respected because different experts have worked on these branches that are based on different philosophies. For example, this branch is based in Phonetic (drawn from Shiksha branch, one of the six parts of Vaidik Vaangmay, the Aaroodh is based on direction occupied by querist, Horoscopy is based in the Raashi rising on East at the time of birth of a person or at the time when querist puts question.

It is said and seen that where the questions relate with some progress, the results are good when the questions begin with G, GH, J, Jh, B, Bh, d, dh, D, Dh.

A few examples will make this clear. It is suggested that with the technological advances like mobile phone that can record discussions, the astrologer may record the audio of question so that analysis, as given below, could be correctly done after the question is made.

Bhaas-haa	Suppose the Sentence begins	Prashnaakshar		GaN	GaN	
		Planet	Remark		Ruler	Remark
Hindi	Aap se jaa-nanaa chaaha-taa …..	Moon	Good	Ra 212	Agni	OK
English	How shall I ……	Sun	OK	Ra 212	Agni	OK
English	For a long time ……	Shani	Not good	Ra 212	Agni	OK
English	Sir, I cannot ……..	Sun	OK	Sa 112	Vaayu	Bad
Maraathi	Malaa phaar divasaa paas-oon	Shani	Not good	Ya 122	Water	Good
Hindi	Kaee dino se ……	Mars	OK	Ja 121	Sun	OK
Hindi	Bacha-pan se aaj tak …….	Shani	Not good	Na 111	Best	THE BEST

Hindi	Jaane Kyaa baat hai ki ….	Budh	OK	Ma 222	Earth	Good
Gujarati	Chhella ek varsh thi ……	Budh	OK	Ma 222	Earth	Good
Gujarati	Naana-paN thi ….	Shukra	Good	Bha 211	Mother	Very good
Gujarati	Evu thaaya chhe ke ….	Moon	Good	Ma 222	Earth	Good
Hindi	Aisaa Hotaa hai ki ……….	Moon	Good	Ma 222	Earth	Good

A few more examples of how general questions begin in Hindi language:-

GaN of Prashn	General Hindi beginnings
Ya GaN (122)	Mahaaraaj, Hamaaraa, Hamesha, Hazaro, Jahaa bhi, Suna Hai,
Ma GaN (222)	Vaise To, Yoon to Mein, Na jaane, Shaadi ke,
Ta GaN (221)	Kaise Bataau, Kaise Kahu, Takleef..,
Ra GaN (212)	Aap to, Share Market, Janm Se, Zindagi, Aap Ka/ Aap se…
Ja GaN (121)	Abhi Tak, Hazaar, Mujhe kaho, Pataa nahi,
Bha GaN (211)	Pandit Ji, Kyaa ab, KaaraN, Shaayad, He Bhagavan.

| Na GaN (111) | Bahut, Ab Tak, Dar Asal, Samajh me…., Kuchh Pataa, |
| Sa GaN (112) | Pichale janm, Pahale to, Ab kyaa, Itane Saal, Sapanaa thaa, Duniya |

Astrologer may explore the answer based on the GaN, and the first sound of any question. It is possible to record the question for recalling and identifying the first sound and GaN because all cell phones have that facility today.

Notes

Notes

Timing An Event

Timing is important from two points of view. Firstly, the questioner may like to ask about likely time of his success etc., and secondly, it is important for the astrologer to know whether the event has already taken place! This becomes more important in Telegnosis because here the short-term events are in focus. This subject is also discussed in Agni puraaN.

In this context, eight directions are considered (excepting Aakaash and Paataal); and the Rulers of these directions are as follows:-

Time	Direction where Sun stays	Special Inference
6 – 9 a.m.	East	King, Kshatriya, Lord Indra with Vajra. (Nature: Kshatriya)
9 – 12 a.m.	Agni (South-west)	Prince, throwable weapons, missiles
12 – 3 p.m.	South	Lord of death with binding weapons (Nature: Vaishya)
3 – 6 p.m.	Nairutya (Southwest)	Bad person with swords etc., in hand

6 – 9 p.m.	West	Good power that attracts others (Nature: Skilled persons)
9 – 12 p.m.	Vaayavya (Northwest)	Power to drag with ballistic weapons
12 – 3 a.m.	North	Good power to physically hit enemy (Nature: Brahmin)
3 – 6 a.m.	Ishaanya (Northeast)	Divine power to win over anything

The direction, where Sun stays, or is passing, is called Deept direction, and indicates that the question belongs to the present times. The direction, behind it is called Angaar, and the direction ahead is called Dhoom; these indicate realization of the question in past and future, respectively.

Suppose, a question is put from East about a promotion at 7 a.m. by a questioner standing in East. Because the Sun is also in East, these indicate good results in near to very near future. But if this question is put from Ishaanya at 7 a.m., it indicates that most probably the person has already appeared in recent past for interview or examination for promotion. And if this question is put from Agni, it means that the interview etc., is yet to be scheduled in near future. In this way, timing an event is possible based on Angaar, Deept and Dhoom nature of directions as measured from position of Sun at the time of question. It is added that the direction exactly opposite to an Angaar, Deept and Dhoom is also treated as same (the 5th direction will have same nature). In other words, in the above case, same results will be predicted if the same question was put at 7 a.m. from West, Nairutya and Vaayavya directions, respectively. This means that there are always, two Shaant directions. In this case, South and North are Shaant directions. Similar explanation is also available in Brihat Samhitaa that says that after three hours of Sunrise, Ishaanya is Mukt Soorya (free of Sun) as East is Praapt Soorya (hosting the Sun).

This method works wonders about LakshaN, taking place in those directions. Suppose in the above example. The querist is seated in East, the time is 7 am, ruled by Sun, and some good song is heard from Agni, indicating travel; this means that the promotion will be on transfer. Based on that, we can know when a LakshaN is likely to show tangible result. This will also be dependent on a LakshaN being observed in Deept, Dhoom and Angaar portions of the Environment.

There is another point to be kept in view. In this style, all three Angaar, Deept and Dhoom are considered as Deept, and the other five are categorized as Shaant (or calm or good). According to one view, Angaar, Deept and Dhoom, though indicate past, present and future, as said above; they indicate presence of fire in some form or other. Some learned people hold that the omens, sighted in these five Shaant districts, unless are expressly good, do not matter. In other words, suppose someone asked a question at 8 a.m. from East about his promotion. The direction and position are dominated by Sun and is indicative of a good success in near future. Suppose at that very moment, a cow is heard crying in pain in East direction, it will tell that the promotion will not be a very good development; but suppose some good music is heard in West, which falls in Shaant district, hence the promotion will be a very profitable affair. The astrologer must decide these based on his own observations. It is for such reasons that an astrologer under Telegnosis, is supposed to be an exceptionally sharp at making observations.

This is strictly about specific questions, and the maximum duration of any horary answers is close to one year. It is also seen that when Lord of Lagn or Aaroodh is Sun the result is seen by 6 months (in one Ayan); if Moon, within 48 Minutes (one KshaN); if Lord is Mangal or Mars, expect result within a Vaasar (a week); if Mercury or Budh, the result will be seen in a Ritu or a season (two months); Jupiter, as a Lord gives results in one month; Shukra will show result in a Paksh (fortnight); and of the Lord is Shani, the result, as said above, will be within one year from that day. Thus, the entire arena of Horary astrology is understood to be for the one year ahead.

If we are guided by Svar Shaastra, the answer will depend on the side from where the question is asked and at that time what Element (Vaayu, Agni, Pruthivi, Jal and Aakaash) was operating. We have discussed that in Right and Left side deal with Sun and Moon and with the features assigned to them; and that the result needs to be announced accordingly. If we are guided by mathematical ways, astrologer gives answer by working out the Dashaa, Antaradashaa and Pratyantara-dashaa, related with lord of the concerned House in a Horo-scope. Suppose, marriage is to be discussed, astrologers will focus on the Lord of 7th House and the strength or otherwise of that House.

Notes

Question – a riddle

Features of a question

As per Bhaashaa Shaastra, a sentence is the verbal communication made at a time, at a place without any unusual breaks in sentences, addressed to someone who understands it in same sense. In this way, question is also a sentence, which is delivered to the astrologer with a specific and respectful request to seek an answer.

Question is a very big subject while studying Communication. We, therefore, will keep it limited to Telegnosis. The very basis of Telegnosis is the question: without a question, there is no answer, there is no Telegnosis. Questions are important everywhere: Doctors, Judges, Police, Politicians, Share-dealers, Farmers, Insurance Companies, and many other experts have their own sets of questions to quickly assess the background before taking a decision. This is reflected also in the Forms, designed by Govt departments for applications. Every application, in this context, is a question paper; and the details provided therein the format, are nothing but verification process. It is necessary also.

Question is generally asked for getting a success. As per analysis, success depends on five things:-
Vansh: This refers to parentage as the person is supposed to

have received genetic qualities from birth. A person born in a rich family and in a poor family start from different points of view, similarly approach of a person born in a literary family does differ from the man born in family of workmen. It is believed that their capability to grasp a subject will be generally in conformity with their parent's lifestyle etc.

Environment: This refers to the facilities available to a person at certain point of time. A singer will shine only when there is an environment to sing and be heard. Suppose the sound system fails in theatre, the music show will fail; maybe the best singer has come to perform.

Opportunity: Not all get opportunity to perform for various reasons. Suppose, X gets tired of repairs, goes home and sleeps for the night, but Y remains at the site where mechanic is able to repair the bus; and is able to reach for Interview next morning.

Effort: It is an essential component of success. X may be a very good painter, but he does not make any effort to approach the King for an appropriate reward.

Time: X and Y are equal in all respects but at the last moment of chess championship, X takes walk over or is not able to reach in time for the Event, and the result is declared due to Time Schedule designed. Similarly, suppose Election Commissioner does not receive the application from the most popular social leader before the cut off time.

With regard to Telegnosis, the question has to be a genuine one, only then the answer can be given. In other words, a question asked with a view to examining the capacity of an astrologer is no question at all because there is no reason to ask that question as such. By just testing the capability of an astrologer, no problem of the querist is going to be resolved. In the same way, the astrologer also should not put a question to himself as a matter of challenge of sort: Again, because the background is defective, there cannot be any answer. We have experienced that we always fail when we answer wasteful question, though we may be partially successful when we want to defend this science of Telegnosis.

With Telegnosis, an astrologer can answer the questions that pertain to any field; even if he has not studied those subjects at all. It is so because the answers are derived by integrated use of more than one style of foretelling, and because all these methods are based on certain principles. We will see the principles behind such methods in this book and will also expect an integrated approach to arrive at an answer. A few gurus believe that astrologers should speak only when there is a question expressed before them, while some believe that it is the duty of astrologer to volunteer the answer whenever required. In different words, Telegnosis is an answering machine that needs to be fed just with a question. Machine does not have expertise of its own, it works on certain principles.

Questions are absent in certain situations e.g., some patients cannot speak, children do not know how to use words to form a question, some people are so terrified as they cannot speak. But even when the questions are not put, it is possible to give answers in most cases. Risht LakshaN are almost vocal answers indicating death, as written in those chapters of Ayurved, and are irrespective of a question being asked or not. But such situations are limited to those extreme medical conditions only, and nowhere else. Therefore, question remains a pre-requisite. Sometimes, a general question is raised during meetings and discussions, these cannot be considered questions because the same are not addressed to any particular astrologer as such; and no answer is awaited in that sense. Thus, the astrologer should know what a question for him is!

Best is the situation where the questions are asked personally. But there are situations where it is not possible, and the questions are put through some representative. Based on our own experience, it is felt that an astrologer must reply all such queries but should not presume a question and volunteer the answer out of compassion. He should wait for question to be presented. It is observed that providing additional information does impress the querist but brings in many other issues that were not in his mind when he came. Let us not plant more question in his mind and start answering the same: They will become your questions more than his. These answers most probably will all go wrong, and will bring a bad name for astrologer, as it amounts flouting of Rules of Astrology.

In the above light, one can feel that the issue of Mushti Prashn is also a fabricated question, and then why that examination be held at all for appointing the best astrologer in the Courts of King! Yes, truly speaking, there is no clear answer, but I feel that there is one genuine situation of appointing the best astrologer in the interests of the Subject of the Kingdom, and further there is no better way than this to assess expertise of the Astrologer candidate. Perhaps for these reasons, the Mushti Prashn for that specific purpose is a genuine Prashn and should be respected.

If there is a question, there has to be an answer to that question. Just one answer. In fact, question and its answer are the two sides of the same coin. But there cannot be just one way to answer any question. Two plus Two is four, and will always be four, whether we write it from right hand or left. It should be same in light of Horoscopy, Horary, LakshaN, Nimitt, Chhaayaa shastra, Numerology or whatever other methods known to us. The querist is concerned with guidance, and not with how it is given. He wants it immediately because he needs to take decision based on astrologers' advice.

Further, the word astrology is not a proper indicator of Jyotish, the term used in India. We have talked about it in some other chapter. Not all may carry Almanac at all points of time, and in such situations, how the astrologer will construct the Chart and study the inter se impact of planets! Not all are good at quick calculations needed to place the planets in those 12 houses and work out the answer. Maybe that much time is not available with the person who put a question. We, therefore, feel that there have to be more methods to predict. The birds and animals do not know mathematics, neither the humans are supposed to know mathematics because it is not the natural language! I therefore hold the view that certainly there is some nonmathematical and nonverbal language that can help humans more than it helps the birds and animals. I am inclined to accept the importance of LakshaN, Nimitt, Chhaayaa, Svar etc., as a basic language to answer a realistic question. We need to apply all these or as many of these as we could. It would get us the best answer as it will enable us to crosscheck our answer there and then.

They claim that a high degree of correlation exists between birth chart and horary chart, but what to do when querist does not know or remember date and time of his birth at all, more so when the relevant Almanac is not readily available with astrologer? Similarly, how will Palmistry be useful if a patient's palm has been imputed, how will Chhaayaa be used in absence of Sunlight or in dim light; how to answer a question put by a 2-year old child or a question posed in a foreign language? Therefore, integrated approach is the best approach, and all astrologers must have first-hand knowledge of all such branches under Jyotish Shaastra. That will only make Telegnosis complete and successful. When we go to a doctor, he uses his stethoscope, goes through our pathological reports, x ray, EEG, ECG, MRI, DNA report etc., in the same way, what is wrong in adopting an integrated approach to answer questions as being discussed here.

Some may argue that veterans like Svami Dayanand Sarasvati have not approved of Astrology. Yes, he has said that reading of Astrological charts etc., is useless, because Vaidik Astrology is intended to guide agricultural operations and medicinal herbs to be used for Yajn etc. These operations were expected to be carried out in conformity with the lunar dates in every season, caused by Earth's orbit in the Solar system. But he has never expressly opposed the LakshaN Shastra (as also obtained in Ayurved, the branch under Rugved), Shakun Shastra (as obtaining in RaamaayaN and Mahabharat) etc. He has not criticized the Muhoort shastra which is part of Atharv Ved for various Yajn. And even if he has differed at times, it only means that he did not approve of application of those branches. He has never discouraged practice of Yog Sootra (It may be added here that Svar shastra is a predictive application derived from Hathayogapradeepika, which can be called Rules if we call Yog Sootra as any Law).

With regard to Telegnosis, it is necessary that any question is expressed very specifically and properly worded without confusion and hesitation. The question should be delivered at a stretch and without breaks as such. If the question is a close ended, answerable in a Yes or a No, it is supposed to be the best question. It shows clarity in the mind of querist which itself is an answer per se. This method of questioning is often seen in Courts of Law where the lawyers spend considerable time in framing questions so that answers from the criminal or the witness are either a Yes or a No. If the questions are not framed nicely, in astrological gamut, it indicates that a clear answer is not destined in that case: as the Computer experts say, 'Garbage in, garbage out'.

Now, let us touch upon some typical questions that were asked to astrologers and are still relevant today. These questions will show the wide spread of Prashn Jyotish in India and will also reveal some aspects of the old lifestyle.

Bhojan Prashn

Sushrut Samhitaa deals with Annarakshaa, where instructions are given as to how the king should protect the harvest of crops so as to preserve the same for a longer period. It is stated that there are such deadly and invisible poisons which, if added to ponds, its water will kill men, trees, and animals because even the dirt on the road becomes poisonous. It is inferred from such texts in Yuktaseneey chapter that there were oral or audio frequencies that could poison even the Chhaayaa of king. This was one reason that Kings preferred to employ such astrologer who could handle such matters in light of Atharv Ved; we may add that in Atharv Ved, poison is also handled with Mantra (Sonography or audio remedies). In this chapter, the Astrologer, who is supposed to be an expert in Agriculture science too, is expected to supervise these operations; and ensure that the food, so preserved for the state, and so cooked for the king in the battlefield, is not poisonous. The main LakshaN of poisonous food are as follows:

- On seeing poisonous food, she-parrot and Cuckoo starts screaming
- On eating poisonous food, the fly dies
- On seeing poisonous food, the crows fly away
- On burning poisonous material in fire, crackling is heard with bursting sparks
- Poison in potable liquid causes lines of varied colour at the surface, and images in it are broken.

In India, such questions came up because the Royal Astrologer was expected to be expert cook on the lines of Ayurvedic lifestyle. He was expected to ensure that the food was not poisonous, and that if at all some issues came up, he was expected to find out everything about food taken in past. Again, the Sages have extended the basic principles of astrology to this sector as summarized below:-

SN.	House from Lagn	Inference drawn
1	1	Person in question (like a king/querist)
2	2	His plate
3	3	Small utensils like spoons in plate (solid)
4	4	Quantity of food and type of host
5	5	Cook, waiters, types of liquid food, served
6	6	Taste, Mood while taking food
7	7	Auxiliary food like salad, pickles

8	8	Quality (fresh or otherwise), dessert if any
9	9	People who eat with querist
10	10	Quantity (whether snacks or full meal)
11	11	Discussions at the time of eating meals
12	12	Rest after meals

Such tables are given almost in all chapters in this compilation where similar indicators are given. It is suggested that the astrologers may take a holistic view of all these factors. For example, with reference to Bhojan Prashn, astrologer is expected to remember the Aaroodh, the LakshaN, the Svar, the Ruling deity, the actions of questioner and the others present on the spot, the tastes indicated by Prashnaakshar etc. at that time. As per one view, if the Ascendant is a fix, movable or common sign, the person has taken food, once, twice and more than two times on that day, respectively. The main taste of food can be ascertained by the Ascendant and its Lord.

Parjanya Prashn (Question on forthcoming monsoon)

As we know, in India, Jyotish has three main branches, GaNit, Phalit and Samhitaa (Muhoort), which mean, Mathematical (GaNit) positions (which will not differ and are called as PramaaN) of rising Raashi as Lagn, and position of planets with degree shown in a Kundali; and the other two branches are dependent on the art of interpretation of such a GaNit (in Kundali); and its use as Electional Astrology (Phalit and Muhoort). Apart from astronomical calculations, man has always made efforts to predict rain for betterment of agricultural crops – the oldest occupation. Seasons are an astronomical fact, but predictions are based on individual interpretation with regard to a question (leading to Kundali or Aaroodh).

I have already written about the Conference held in the first week of June 1998 in Junagadh campus of Agriculture University where scientists and astrologers were invited to submit papers on the forthcoming Monsoon, and the selected few were presented. A gentleman from Jamnagar, a lawyer by profession and a scholar of Astrology by choice, took the stage at about 10.15 and as he started reading his paper, it started raining outside. It was the very first shower of that season in Gujarat. I am citing this fact to show that there exist many other methods to predict rains. The wild and domestic animals, insects like fly and ants, the birds, almost all know how good the next monsoon would be, whether they are able to speak like us or not. They know. When I talked to those scholars, I came to know that most of them had heavily depend on the non-mathematical ways of foretelling. In India, Bhadali and Ghaag are the two prominent names who have given invaluable clue to rains in local languages which is about one thousand year old. They have spoken of direction of wind on important days like Holi, Aashaadhi Dviteeya and Akshay Truteeya; and we have included those LakshaN of Monsoon and instant rains in this compilation as a ready-reckoner.

Varah Mihir and Paraashar were the two main Rishis who worked on Parjanya (Rains) and compiled invaluable evidence with regard to these matters. It is seen that the possibilities of major cyclones, hurricanes and storms are much more either before or after the PoorNima or Amaavasyaa.

 Telegnosis

No one could be against use of machines but let us not play down the questions by ignoring the visible facts like these. In ancient India, it is said that it takes six months to deliver the Garbh (rain-foetus), in other words, each rainy cloud is conceived before six months. This conception generally starts in the bright half of November or December every year. If it was conceived in night, it would rain during the night or otherwise. They have also said that the Solar Maxima has close relation with Monsoon. Today, the scientists agree with this correlation. It is said that the Maxima emits electric charge on upper layers of Earth's atmosphere which either results in snow or water. This electric charge also causes mass movement of airmass, causing storms of sorts. While all accept these atmospheric changes, no one really knows why Sunspots appear after every decade!

Varah Mihir says that for healthy conception of Rains, the following factors are noted:-
1. Wind blowing from North, Ishaanya and East
2. A smoky circle around Moon or Sun during winter
3. If Rainbow appears in East much before Monsoon
4. Dark blue sky in winter
5. Needle sharp ends of newly formed clouds, that appear red in light of the rising and setting Sun
6. Prati Soorya is seen in North, East or South (Prati Soorya is called Mock Sun which means that Sun shining through thick layers of clouds but is seen to be present at some other place than where it is supposed to be at that hour. Similarly, there are Prati Chandra, seen in night)
7. He notes that appearance of Dhoomaketu (Comet), Ulkaapaat (fall of meteorite), eclipse, Sunspots too much of lightening in winter are indicators of poor monsoon. He says that if Rainbow appears in East during monsoon,

it will reduce the showers considerably.

Following are indicators of rains (during Monsoon) on day of question
1. If morning Sun is extremely bright
2. If taste of stored water becomes slightly acrid
3. If shape of the rainy clouds is like a black and white python
4. If fish tries to jump out of water
5. If ants start shifting to higher places in the house or compound
6. If cat starts scratching the ground
7. If snake tries to climb trees
8. If cows want to run to their calves
9. If salt becomes moist
10. If there is a red circle around Moon
11. If donkeys start running suddenly and when their ears have become tightly held upward

While answering question on rains, in addition to these LakshaNs, the following are also equally important good omens as per my discussions with many foretellers:-
1. If a young girl arrives
2. If someone brings a pot full of water or some good liquid
3. If a learned or pious person arrives
4. If someone touches genitals
5. If topic of waterbodies is suddenly brought up by some stranger
6. If the Prashnaakshar begins with G Gh, J Jh, D Dh, D DH, B Bh.

Rain was measured by King in terms of DroN. One DroN is equal 4 Aadhak (one Aadhak is a circular pot 8-inch deep having 20-inch diameter). 4 DroN rain is considered as the best rain.

While the Ulkaapaat, Thunderbolts, Wind Velocity, and Sunspot etc., foretell bad monsoon and hence tough time ahead, there are a few more such warnings to be issued by the astrologer to the administrator (when asked) for a period of ten months, as a part of his moral duty. The following signs relate to the King or the head of the Country:-

1. When Festoons and flags on temple, palace, Court, catch fire for no reason
2. When trees fall automatically, though they are not old
3. When trees produce sound like drums
4. When no crop grows despite irrigation
5. When crops mature before the due date
6. When nocturnal creature keeps coming out in daytime and roam; and otherwise
7. When forest birds fly to cities and stay, and city birds fly out
8. When cow starts sneezing (this also indicates certain death in case of question relating longevity)

Koop Prashn

With regard to Koop Prashn, it may be mentioned that it is part of Vaastu Shaastra where the head of Vaastupurush is imagined in the Ishaanya direction. He is imagined as a sleeping person with his head down. For this reason, the astrologer is expected to make 12 equal parts like a horoscope made on that piece of land and suggest digging of a Koop (a vaapika or a well) in the East or North side of Vaastupurush.

Groundwater, quantity and quality, is seen from the 4th House, running water is seen from 7th House and the 10th

House is to be examined (if question is put by King or his representative) for rains in the area of querist. Depending of the Raashi Tattv (e.g., Vaayu) shows taste of water, possibility of a storm etc.

Surati Prashn

Like the Bhojan Prashn, the scope of Surati Prashn is also limited to love affairs of administrators. In today's life, this tool could be used for cross-examination in court cases to short-list the criminal activities. While the other aspects like Aaroodh, LakshaN, Svar remain common, the 7th House and its Lord show the possibility of a coitus. The degree of Moon or Aaroodh indicates the age of the female. In other words, if the degree of Moon is between 20 and 30, the woman must be young, if less than that, it may indicate an underage or a weak girl; and if more than that, an old or mature woman is indicated. In case the querist is a woman, the moon or Mangal, whichever is stronger, may indicate age of the male.

Nasht Prashn/ Jaatak

This term is used for two types of questions. First type shows that the question is too theoretical or is asked to test or mislead the astrologer: Such a question is also called a Nasht Prashn. Secondly, the question is asked to find out a lost person or an article. It is said that the questions falling in purview of the first type are generally asked when the astrologer is breathing through SushumNaa, or both nostrils. It, therefore, is better not to answer those questions and politely decline from answering those questions.

Further, whenever discussion is centred around a missing person, the same thing is called Nasht Jaatak, and when an article is missing, they call it Nasht Prashn.

As regards the second type of Nasht Prashn, in addition to other methods, astrologer should examine the following:

1. If Aaroodh is Char (Movable), the articles or kidnapped person has been shifted to a far off place. Suppose Shani is in movable Raashi, the prisoner will be moved or released. Char Aaroodh also shows that the thief is not from the family;

2. If Aaroodh if Sthir, the articles or kidnapped person is somewhere around the original place; Sthir Aaroodh also shows that the thief is a family member;

3. If it is a mixed sign, it is not very far from the place, but cannot be predicted certainly; Common sign in Aaroodh shows that the thief is in neighbourhood;

4. If Moon or Jupiter are seated in Aaroodh, the question about life and death of a person;

5. If Shani is seated or is related with 6, 8 and 12 House, it is related to theft;

6. If querist had touched Dark half while finding Aaroodh, the event took place in night, and vice versa;

7. Suppose, the Lord of a movable Aaroodh or Lagn is in Baal avasthaa, say that he is travelling but has not gone far;

8. If nonvegetarian birds and animals are seen ahead of the querist, it is possible that the lost person is alive and will be located, but if they are behind the querist, the lost person is perhaps not alive;

9. If the querist touches his Right side body, preferably some good limb, the lost article or person will be found, and vice versa;

10. If during the discussion, good and accceptable smell, words or music are noticed, the result will be favourable, and not otherwise;

11. A principle based approach will always pay, for example,

the Lord of Lagn (1st House) will be a receiver and the Lord of 11th House will always be a giver; hence astrologer should examine such aspects before finally announcing result;

12. If the querist touches any of his internal limbs like tooth, the thief is from within the family;

13. If he touches his toe/ toes, the thief is one of the subordinates;

14. If he touches his thumb/ fingers, the thief could be one of sons/ daughters;

15. If he feels his naval point, the mother or the real brother could be the thief;

16. The object will not be realised, if querist first touches internal organs and immediately touches the external organs;

17. If immediately after asking question, the querist uses toilet, spits, throws something, the object will not be realised; and

18. Prashn Gyaan suggests that if Lord of 7th House is Mars, the thief could be a child; if Budh, a boy; if Guru, a mature person; if Shukra, a young person; if Saturn/ Rahu, a very aged and cunning person; if Sun, a middle aged person; and if Moon, an old person could be the thief or culprit.

Marriage and Children

For marriage, 5th House indicates possibility of Love marriage and the 7th House indicates type of partnership and appearance of partner. In addition to Kundali, Svar etc., the following LakshaN should be taken in view while answering the questions related to marriage. In India, marriage is interpreted as companionship with one spouse and anything outside this is seen as irregular. If at the time of question, a man appears with two women or if a woman enters with two men; predict remarriage or presence of more than one spouse.

If the question is related with the gender of the foetus, the astrologer should examine the 5th House of the father of the child and 9th House of the mother of the child (the pregnant woman). If the Aaroodh, its lord is in Male Raashi, the child will be a male, if the Aaroodh and its lord are in Female Raashi, the child will be a female; if the Aaroodh is neither male not female, predict uncertain delivery of child or a eunuch. If in a Kundali, Guru is in odd Raashi, predict birth of a son; if Shukra is in even Raashi, predict a daughter; and if Guru is in a common Raashi, predict twins.

It is seen that if the question is presented during the day time, and the Ascendant is powerful and is occupied by bright and good planets, the woman will deliver child during day time, otherwise in the night hours.

If a young girl or a boy enters the scene, the marriage can be predicted for a boy or a girl and the appearance of the groom and bride will match with these new entrants. If the querist touches right or left side of his body, the male and female child, respectively, are to be predicted. If astrologer happens to SEE a pregnant woman, (a person in need of promotion or benefits) from the side where is breath is, know (do not predict in words) the delivery of a son and success etc, otherwise a daughter; but if a question is PUT, predict as per breath: suppose the astrologer is breathing from Right nostril and a question put from Left side that 'whether I will get a son or a daughter?' the answer will be daughter because the first choice will be answer if question comes from the fuller side, and the second choice will be the answer if question is put from the vacuum side. It is added that while dealing with a question on birth of child, if astrologer notices voice of a male more so on the right side, more so in presence of people in odd number; predict birth of a male child, and vice versa.

In Astrology, presence of herb and its condition and placement do form part of answer to a query. In astrology, and Vaastu shaastra, it is said that if a person has fruit bearing trees in the residential area, occupied by him, there are obstacles either in career of children or some other serious issues relating childbirth. I like to cite an example of my own life. I leave it to the reader whether to treat this as an observation or as a mere coincident! A leading and rich businessman in Dehradun could get his both sons married within a week after respectfully transferring all fruit bearing trees, planted in his foreyard for years. I have seen that by way of a daily TarpaN to the Vaastu Devataa, makes good difference in such cases: We all know that Vaastupurush is supposed be sleeping from Ishaanya to Nairutya, with head down in Ishaanya. As remedial measures, we can suggest that when the problem of children and marriage is concerned, better to remove some trees, or replace them by good flower plants or some good ornamental trees. A small list of important LakshaNs is given below for a ready reference :-
- If there is a thorny tree within compound, enemies are always powerful,
- If there are such trees that lactate, thief is more powerful,
- Fruit-bearing trees in compound are harmful for marriage/ career of children,
- If immediate neighbour is temple, there will be mental disorder in the family,
- If trees are full of ant-hills, calamities continue to descend on that family; and

- If there is a tree in an elevated terrain in the middle of that place, fear of thieves.

Yuddh Prashn

This type of questions is generally asked by kings, administrators, lawyers and criminals who want to bring a result to their advantage. The astrologer should decide whether his answers will add to the good of his society, otherwise, it is better to leave the matter. Astrologer should not guide the miscreants. In a Yuddh Prashn, like in other cases, astrologer is expected to conduct the same procedure of taking Aaroodh, check Svar, LakshaN etc., and then answer the question. It is to be remembered that answers given to King and his Military officials are generally relevant to the country.

Yuddh Prashn are discussed in all books on astrology as well as in AgnipuraaN. In Yuddh Prashn, astrologer should advice beginning of war in Sheershoday Lagn, preferably in Vijay Muhoort, best if during the Hora, ruled by the Lagn; and when breath of King and General is in Right nostril. The army should be advised to reach the battlefield non-stop. As regards LakshaN, the astrologer should note that nonvegetarian birds and animals, if seen ahead of the army, it is good as it indicates that Nature has arranged for their food in anticipation of success of this army. If the nonvegetarian birds and animals are seen behind the army, it indicates that Nature wants to consume this army itself.

The following LakshaN are special to Yuddh Prashn:-

1. If the querist stands on right leg and shakes weapon or right hand, victory can be predicted
2. If there is an effort to burn lamp or put on electric bulb etc., the result will be good

3. If someone brings out subject of weapons, more so on the side of astrologer's breath, result will be good

4. If someone talks of compromise or stopping the war, better ask not to go for war

5. Enemy attacks from the side from where crows enter the kingdom, or fort or city

6. If crows fly from behind and drop flesh near front row, it is good, and vice versa

7. If dog leads the army, defeat is foretold

8. If dog stands and blocks the road, expect some theft or dacoity or attack on way

9. If strong wind blows from front, it is indication of resistance in army's march, and vice versa

10. If horses and elephants do not march and resist, better to postpone time of war.

It is suggested that the above questions may sound to be outdated, but it is likely that the above guidance would be useful in answering all those questions that are extension of the above or where only the outer layer has changed. We may have to think of a truck or a tank or a scooter in place of a house, an elephant or a dog as per the situation. A black vehicle could be a changed form of Yamaraaj. We need to note that astrology remains art of interpretations, and we will have to be good at the basic principles. Simply because the outer shapes of so many objects have changed with passage of time, the utility or context of the same does not change. Everything continues to exist as a LakshaN for an astrologer.

With regard to Bhaav in the Kundali for Yuddh Prashn, the twelve Houses, indicate, the King, King's treasure, his military strength, size of his army, the ambassador or representative abroad, the Enemy (6th House), communication in battle field, Victory or defeat, Decision making skill of the king, Business affairs in Kingdom, Income of Taxes in the Treasury, and from the 12th House, we see the expenditure of King on various aspects of administration.

Notes

Notes

Illustration

1. Suppose it is 9 a.m., and you are seated inside your house facing East on 20 January 2023, and the querist comes
   - If you see him directly – better
   - If someone announces his arrival – indicates some delay in result
2. Examine your breath, when he is coming
   - If he is on your fuller nostril, better
   - If he is on your non-working nostril, not good
   - If you are breathing from both nostrils, predict failure
3. Observe his dress, confidence, smell, appearance
   - If dress etc., are clean, better; if dirty, not good, smeared, bad
4. Observe querist silently from the point of view of Touch Analysis.
5. Hear his question
   - If presented confidently, predict good.
   - If presented with breaks, predict interruptions.
   - If presented with pathos, predict unfavorable results
6. Recall or jot down the GaN and Prashnaakshar
   - Recall the chapter on Prashnaakshar and make note of formation of sentence
7. Keep observing LakshaN around as discussed in the relevant chapter.

8. **KUNDALI**

   Method 1: Remember that, today, Sun will be in Makar Raashi, and will be in 12th House, so it will be a Mesh Lagn Kundali, with Lord of 5th in 12th House.

   Method 2: Show a blank Horoscope to querist and ask him to draw on a blank paper or soil and ask him to place his hand in any one of those 12 Houses. Note the House where he places his finger. Either take that as Lagn or place Moon in that House. Results will be similar, if not same.

   Method 3: Note the direction faced by the querist. Find our Lagn based on where he is seated. If he is concentrating on any object around him, observe that direction as Lagn, and ignore direction where has come from. Refer to the Table given in this compilation where the 12 Raashi are assigned to the 8 directions.

   Now, after arriving at the Lagn, place Sun and Moon and the other planets as per their current position obtaining in the Almanac or any good source of such information
   - Check whether the Aaroodh is in Moveable Rashi or immoveable or Common
   - Check whether Aaroodh is Sheershoday (good), or Prushtoday or Ubhayoday
   - Check whether Lord of Aaroodh or selected Bhaav is between 2 malefic planets
   - The stage comes to ascertain the strength of the 12 Houses (Bhaav) and make study of the House, pointed out or indicated by the querist as said above
   - Use torn pieces of newspapers, tree twigs, available flowers, etc., as said in the relevant chapter for ascer-

taining strength of Bhaav or otherwise;

9. Light a Lamp or ask him to light, and observe as discussed in the relevant chapter.
10. Observe the Chhaayaa of the querist if it denotes something.
11. Compare the Kundali made by you as said above with any Kundali presented by querist as reference.
12. Ask the querist to give a 3-digit number (1 through 8) and interpret as given in the relevant chapter.

The above will bring to fore the answer (success or otherwise) to the issue presented by the querist. Maybe astrologer might miss some of the above answers, but Telegnosis opens opportunities to examine the matter considering multiple ways, and which obviously is more scientific and reliable than arriving at answer just by using any one of the above methods.

Notes

Notes

Mushti Prashn & A Myth

Few know that astrologers were put to stringent tests before appointment in the Royal Courts. In the old days in Bhaarat, Kings used to have two main assistants viz., the Prime Minister and the Chief Advisor. While the Prime Minister was the administrator of everything, and almost everything was decided in the light of what the Advisor threw. Maybe prime minister was more visible, but the role of advisor was never underestimated. Advisor used to be an expert in Medicine, Ved and Upanishads, Neeti Shaastra, Krushi - Agriculture, all branches of foretelling including horoscopy, more popularly known as Astrology, today; and also used to be in charge of Justice, timing the implementation of various Schemes and Wars; and other important meetings of the King. He was expected to supervise the Security of royal kitchen and the food preservation for the State. Due to such vast practicable knowledge, his role was very important for the kings.

Strictly speaking, Indian Vedic literature is seen as Three Ved viz, Rugved, Yajurved and Saamaved. Though Maharshi Ved Vyas edited the literature into four, by adding Atharv Ved, many scholars omit the last one because it also deals with Yaatu. Yaatu refers to magic caused by doing various procedures. Shukla Yaatu, and KrishN Yaatu are the two types of Yaatu. For this reason, the Kings used to prefer appointing an Advisor who has thorough knowledge of KrishN Yaatu of Atharv Ved.

Before appointing Advisor, a test was conducted which is known as Mushti Prashn. Here a querist, generally the King, used to pick up a small object without being seen; and hold it in his tightly closed fist (Mushti) so that no part of that object is visible even to him. The candidates, seated in distant room, were, then, called one after the other. They were expected to instantly tell the colour, odour, shape, taste etc., of the object in the King's fist. King could allow five or seven attempts as per his desire. The candidate who defined the object to its closest form was appointed as the Royal Advisor.

No time lag was allowed to candidates to calculate or think while answering the question. I do not think there can be any comparable examination of any subject anywhere in the world. It is therefore not necessary to say anything about the high calibre of such successful candidates. Thus, the Advisor was supposed to know multiple ways of foretelling. He was expected to be wonderful at Arithmetical calculations, Svar, Horoscopy, LakshaN, Shaareer chapters of Ayurved, and many more branches of knowledge which were in existence at that time. Telegnosis is an effort to connect today's astrologers and scholars with the same tradition.

I have heard this from my Gurus. This looks tough, but I also know a few gentlemen who can do this: They answer the moment last letter of the question stands delivered. But I have not seen any professional astrologers aware of a Mushti Prashn, which was the ultimate test of an astrologer.

What I want to highlight here is that we also need to know

multiple ways of foretelling for two main reasons. First, the language of Nature is not and cannot be mathematics, and that horoscopy is largely a mathematical exercise based on man-made assumptions; and secondly, the Nature seems to be well understood by animals, other than humans as we see their behaviour during the Natural Calamities. They are able to prepare for life saving arrangements. In other words, Nature speaks its own language which is perceivable through our five sensory organs: Eye, Ear, Skin, Taste and fragrance. The more a foreteller knows about these organs and their abilities, the better he would be as a foreteller. In Vedic parlance, astrologer should be able to answer based on Gaatra-VeeNa (body of a person as a musical instrument). In other words, what the body of the person, putting a question, is speaking or singing. I can cite an example, a mathematician cum foreteller can smell a serpent in your compound even during the dark night! He says that when a dog can trace the thief based on smell of his perspiration, why it should be impossible for a human being to extend his 'nose' to that extent. He says Bhaarat has devised such meditational practices which train our sensory organs to sense beyond the normal band of colours, the vibrations of sound and light; and a hundred things like that.

Mushti Prashn expects the foreteller to decode everything around him. He should be able to scan the environment around him and segregate the same into basic five elements of Nature viz., Akash (Ether), Vayu (gad or wind), Agni (Fire), Jal (Water) and Prithivi (Earth or soil). Each has main feature viz., Akash indicates place, room, various colours, possibility of holding everything; Vayu indicates any gaseous form, lateral movement, any frequency whether that of light or sound, a mix of colours, mainly blue or black, and old age;

Fire stands for upward movement, creation, red colour, bile, youth, energy, ability to change forms of object; Water speaks for beauty, feminine nature, softness, white colour, downward and quick movements; and Prithvi stands for Yellow colour, firmness, circular shapes, routine matters etc. These are just some illustrative features of these five elements. To be a good reader of Nature to foretell a particular happening, one has to make this illustrative list longer by personal experiments in light of what the Sages have left behind. Our Ayurved, at many places praises instincts of animals, particularly of female species. The female species of animals seem to be improved versions in most ways because they, from the very inception, are supposed to be instrumental in leading Life to a newer height. They are more gifted with ability to interpret the Nature and while saving themselves and the family from natural disasters. For such reasons, Sanskrit literature is full of praise for housewives to be respected as deity; I think there is no parallel to this concept in any other civilizations as on date.

Very close to Mushti Prashn is the concept of answering genuine questions put before the saints in solitary places like Himaalay. Naturally, they stay without any Almanac or any comparable source to indicate positions of Planets in sky at any point of time. They, in addition to their spiritual powers, must be applying some of these methods that decode the language of Nature. I may be permitted to say that Telegnosis is a science of sorts and it is not necessary that the astrologer should be a spiritual person in the strict sense.

Bhagavan Kaartikey and GaNesh – Facts of Astrology
There are various types of Astrology dating from 1800 BC till date as per information available on Internet. As per Indian

view, we see it included in RaamaayaN in a very systematic form for more than 500 astrological references. RaamaayaN is at least as old as 12000 BC - as mathematically and astronomically proved by Dr. Nilesh Oak of US. In view of that, this science, whether in India or elsewhere, is in human hands for about 20000 years now!

In all countries and all civilisations, astrology has been a decision-making tool in differing ways. Experts in all these branches claim to be perfect in their predictions and many of them generate good earnings from this as a business. Almost all astrologers seem to be throwing a challenge that their predictions are always true. Be that so for a better society, but there is nothing wrong in accepting that nothing is cent percent correct. Novices make wonderful predictions and many masters go wrong every now and then.

I am reminded of a story, told by my ancestors that keeps me under control whenever I am overconfident. The story is very indicative, though imaginary. In India, we have a tradition to use mythological and historical characters to present our own views either in form of a drama or in poetry. This story in on the same lines. Bhagavan Shankar and Mother Paarvati have two sons. Bhagavan Kaartikey was the elder brother of Ganesh ji. Shankar ji, with a view to studying the accuracy and usefulness of Astrology, called both his sons, and asked them to go around entire Universe; and report to him about the veracity of predictive methods. Ganesh ji was the younger one, so he was given study of predictions based on Natal charts, popularly known as horoscopes; and Bhagavan Kaartikey, being the elder son, was entrusted with the other branches of making predictions like Chhaayaa (Aura), LakshaN, Shakun (Shagun/ Shukan), Nimitta, Svar, Ank (Numerology) and Kinesics (body language including palmistry, facial structure etc.)

Both started journey in opposite directions and returned after some time. Bhagavaan Shankar called them and asked about the efficiency of these methods. Bhagavaan Kaartikey said that based on his experience, the predictions came true only to the extent of 33%, Ganesh Ji also said that his predictions, based on horoscopy, generally came true to that extent i.e., 33%! This story is to tell us that even if a human being is a combine of Bhagavaan Kaartikey and Ganesh, the accuracy would be 66%; and anything beyond would be only a God's gift.

Notes

Overviews

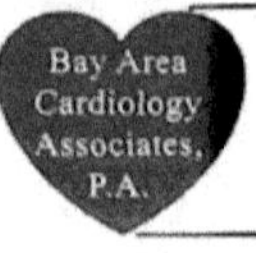

Ravi N. Khant, M.D., F.A.C.C	Saurabh K. Chokshi, M.D., F.A.C.C.
Stephen W. Mester, M.D., F.A.C.C	William J. Bugni, M.D., F.A.C.C
Robert M. Betzu, M.D., F.A.C.C	Robert M. Dewhurst, M.D., F.A.C.C.
Tehreen Khan, M.D., F.A.C.C.	Umesh Gowda, M.D., F.A.C.C.
Chris Perzanowski, M.D., F.A.C.C.	Juna Misiri, M.D., F.A.C.C.
Umesh Tamhane, M.D., F.A.C.C.	Vamsi Gaddipati, M.D., F.A.C.C.

Consultative, Diagnostic, & Interventional Cardiology
Diplomats of American Board of Cardiovascular Disease

September 2022

RE: Telegnosis-Preliminary Feasibility study

Dear Mr. Raval,

Thank you very much for allowing me to participate in the Telegnosis Preliminary Feasibility study. I collected data on 20 patients and compared them to your diagnosis and treatment plan (without revealing the patient's name but only by being next to the patient and sending you age and race data). Even though the sample size was small, and the results were variable, the accuracy of diagnosis was nearly 90-95% in some cases. Based on your diagnosis, I formulated a plan of care for several patients with excellent health benefits.

Of course, we need a large patient pool to study this; further, I see promise in this modality (with no healthcare cost attached) if combined with modern medicine.

I sincerely acknowledge Dr. Arati Shah-Yukich's generous efforts in coordinating the study and Dr. Melinda Toney's tireless work and wisdom as my co-investigator. Through several discussions on the topic, I learned a lot about this ancient diagnostic technique (like Ayurveda and traditional Chinese medicine-TCM), and I am indebted.

Sincerely,

Saurabh Chokshi, MD MBA FACC, RPVI
Asst. Prof. Medicine and Cardiology, University of South Florida,
Past Director of Cardiac Cath Lab, Tampa General Hospital
Founding Partner, Bay Area Cardiology Associates, Tampa Bay Area

Melinda Q. Toney, MD

17 Scenic View Drive, Weaverville, NC 28787

www.AwakenChrysalis.com

info@AwakenChrysalis.com

Phone (828) 552-4276 | FAX (877) 479-3951

January 3, 2023

Dear Mr. Raval,

I am deeply grateful to you and Dr. Arati Shah-Yukich for the privilege of being a part of the Preliminary Telegnosis Feasibility Study. You graciously provided Telegnosis readings remotely for each of the 16 cases, most of whom are my patients in my Integrative Medical practice, some of whom are friends and family whose medical records were accessible to me. I provided you with their initials, age and gender while I was in their presence either in person or remotely by video call. In my initial interview with each case, I asked them what they would like to know about their health and their life circumstances to help them make wise medical or life choices ahead. Since I have a holistic approach as a medical doctor, my patients and friends are well aware that their health situation is often a reflection of their life perspective and circumstances.

I submitted their and my questions to you, to which you

kindly and tirelessly responded. I had a meeting with each one to give share with them your initial readings and your readings prompted by their questions. Often you and I had dynamic exchanges about each case to help clarify the patient's circumstances to explore and zoom into nature's signals via Telegnosis information to aid us in the path forward. The results were variable, the highest of 75% accuracy for the items on each initial reading matching the patient's current situation, but many items seemed impertinent at the time. Since it appeared that time had to pass in order to reveal many of the Telegnosis reading items, more questions were posed and case review after time passed to see if any of the readings bore true with time.

I am writing to you one year since we started this Telegnosis exploration to see the long-term revelations. Although the follow-up reviews have not been complete, some of the Telegnosis readings came true with time.

At this point, I believe that there was enough resonance between the readings and the circumstances that bore out, that warrants further exploration. It is my impression that by looking at the signs of nature to serve a person's health and life path, the holistic art of Telegnosis could bring many useful gifts. This hypothesis could be proven with refinement of exactly how to use the data of the readings in a practical manner. In this initial exploration, many influencing factors arose that bear further examination to come to this refinement. Some of the factors include: the consciousness of the Telegnosis practitioner, the doctor, and the patient; choosing pertinent data from the big picture that Telegnosis provides as applicable to the particular questions that the doctor and patient think would serve; posing pertinent questions to serve the patient's path.

Cultural / language differences in communicating such deep issues. This is like finding a needle in a big haystack! But now that Telegnosis has come to the fore in these times and the question of it's service to mankind is posed, there must be an answer! Although the answer could take much time and effort, I believe that those who are called to explore this intrigue will be refined through the process.

The task of creating a bridge between the holistic view of nature and the binary approach of current scientific approach (in particular conventional medicine) is huge. However, in my view, this is actually the task at hand for humanity as a whole in its current condition! We are being invited to expand our minds and our hearts to find our way as a human race. Further collaboration in the exploration of Telegnosis is part of this movement of creating a bridge between the big picture and the small picture. As we refine ourselves we will come to the point that by breathing between the two worlds, in each of us the two worlds become One!

I pray that these offerings serve your endeavours to bring the gifts of Telegnosis to serve humanity at this pivotal time!

With Deep Respect and Gratitude,

Melinda Q. Toney, M.D.
Family Medicine
Board Certified in Integrative Medicine
Founder of Awaken Chrysalis

Author's Other Publications

Pighalatee Barf, Hindi Urdu Poetry (1981), Preface by Harivanshray Bachchan, Kaifi Azmi and Hasrat Jaipuri.

Gujarati Poetry (2009).

Collection of Hindi Urdu Poetry (2011)

Indian Philosophy, including all viewpoints in a nutshell. (2021)

A Triangular Circle (2024)

Gujarati Translation of Telegnosis, Published under National Education Policy, Adopted by GTU (2024)

We Are Not the Same

Bettina Soto

India | USA | UK